Confessions of a

by Lyndo

C000139469

Contents

Introduction

Dream job? Does flying around the world to inspect hotels and getting paid at the same time sound too good to be true? From the glamour of lying on Caribbean beaches to being face to face with a gunman, this is my story as I travelled around South America, North Africa and Europe auditing hotels, and my story intends to give an insight into the reality of living and working in foreign countries, whilst experiencing things that could prove invaluable if you are thinking of 'seeing the world' or that working abroad is your 'dream job'.

Around the world there are people checking hotels to ensure that they are safe for your wellbeing whilst away enjoying yourselves on holiday or working away on business. But what about the auditor and their experiences, the good, the bad and the dangerous, that they go through travelling around the globe, alone, to carry out this work.

I have worked for various tour operators and suppliers to the leisure industry, but I will not name any of them who are still operating in this book, hence why I refer to them as the 'UK company' only. The reason I decided to write this publication is to give readers the good, the bad, the funny and sometimes the dangerous experiences of travelling abroad whilst trying to earn a living.

After serving 10 years in the Armed forces, I spent around 15 years in the tour operator/ hotel industry as a Health and Safety Manager.

The role I carried out was to audit hotels to ensure that the safety standards were in line with recommended guidelines that are recognised (but sometimes ignored!) the world over.

As an indication of the depth of the audit, it has over 600 questions and I have listed a few of the procedures/ standards that are checked in each hotel to give you an idea what I was auditing:

Kitchen – delivery areas, storage, food temperatures (before and during cooking including reheating, serving and holding), cleanliness, hygiene and kitchen maintenance.

Fire precautions – fire alarm, testing, staff training, fire exits and doors, smoking policy, extinguishers, sprinklers, practice evacuations, emergency lighting and signage.

Swimming pool – Water quality, chemical content, testing, signage, cleaning, pool plant equipment, lifeguards, separation from children's pools and general pool condition.

Gas - boiler rooms, carbon monoxide, flue gasses in relation to bedrooms, emergency procedures.

Bedrooms – Fire doors, emergency signage, the balcony height and construction (balconies with ladder type balustrades, largely spaced apart or are too low invite trouble)

General – trip hazards, children's clubs/ play areas, legionella controls and electrical safety.

The hotels ranged from city centre budget hotels to 5* all-inclusive beach resorts, with everything in between.

I generally travelled just out of season, especially to beach resorts, and have lost count of how many flights, hire cars and hotel stays I have had, as well as how many times I've got lost! The flights, hotels and appointments were all pre-booked by 'the UK company' and at times it felt like they should all go on a logistics and geography course.

I am not from Liverpool, but I was brought up within 10 miles of Liverpool Football club so anyone who isn't local to me, including those I met in the Armed Forces, incorrectly called me a 'scouser' as to everyone else I 'sound' like I am from Liverpool, so if I was 5000 miles away in Colombia, a 'yes, I am from Liverpool' was far easier to explain. I also learnt that the world seems to have a fascination with the Liverpool football player, Mo Salah. The language barrier around the world, when you only speak English, was evidently a problem but I somehow managed to muddle through with a mix of crazy hand gestures and a very useful translator app. This book details my experiences whilst working abroad, in country order which is not necessarily the order they were completed and are my personal views only, however no doubt others will have been to the same places and have completely different views.

I would like to thank friends and family for helping me put this book together, especially my beautiful wife who has fully supported me during the whole process of working abroad and writing this publication.

Chapter 1

Colombia

'We are not sure exactly where you are going yet, but it's definitely somewhere in South America and you're going on Friday for 3 weeks' was my somewhat unhelpful brief for my upcoming trip. Ok, I thought, I have never been there so why not. When else would I get the opportunity to visit these countries and get paid at the same time? Surely this would be fun, right? Where I was exactly going was only confirmed 2 days before I left, giving me just enough time to check that the flights, hotels, audits all matched, and of course time to pack.

The first issue was how complex (and looking back now, how ridiculous) the planned itinerary was. It was 16 flights, over 21 days, with 12 different hotels, 12 different hire cars, all in 5 different countries (Colombia, Ecuador, Peru, Uruguay, and Paraguay). Half of the flights were in the early morning so a 5.30am flight meant I was up at 2am to get to the airport, which as a one off is fine but doing this 4-5 times on the run whilst working during the day was obviously going to be very difficult. Some days I had 3 flights, all with different airlines which meant rechecking in at each airport. It also did not allow for any breathing space between flights and I did raise this concern because if you missed one flight, the domino effect that could cause on future flights, audits etc would be problematic but I was assured it would be ok. I only had 1 planned weekend off and on all the other days I was either working or flying. I was now under no illusion that this was going to be easy, but by far I underestimated how demanding this was going to be. The effect of constantly flying, working, the heat and humidity and eating different types of food has on your body cannot be a good one. Add to this the language barrier as well as the general stress of working and this was never going to be 'fun' but I was still looking forward to it and wherever I have been I always tried to embrace these differences and try to turn them into positive experiences. This though turned out to be the most difficult, dangerous, and demanding trip I have been on to date.

It was also a good job I checked the itinerary, as the plan on one of the days was to get a 5am flight, then carry out a 10am, 1pm and a 4pm audit before getting on another flight at 8pm, which was obviously going to be a tough day. After investigating the finer details, it transpired that the 1pm audit was going to be a 300-mile drive away from the first one, then I would have needed to board a motorized canoe for 2 hours through the Amazon! Once highlighted, this audit was obviously cancelled but this did prove why it is so important to double check the plan! I also think that someone in the office would have benefited from a Geography lesson.

After saying my goodbyes at home and leaving my car at the airport I boarded a late morning flight to Frankfurt in Germany for a short stopover before boarding my 12-hour flight to my first stop on my trip to the capital of Colombia, Bogota. To sit on a long flight, next to a non-English speaking fellow passenger is a strange experience even though I enjoy flying. Without any conversation you go through various stages of the flight, the relaxation stage with films, food and drinks, before the sleep stage, then the boredom stage before the lonely and 'already missing home' stage. Then you eat and drink again. Then you check the time and after all that you still have 5 ½ hours to go before you land. How you cope with this when you do not enjoy flying, I imagine, is an altogether different experience.

Bogota

After eventually landing at about 9pm and collecting my luggage, I changed some currency and obtained a local sim card for my phone and proceeded to the arrival lounge to collect my hire car, but suddenly I did not feel right. I was dizzy, disoriented and felt lightheaded and to be honest I could have thrown up at any point. I bought some water and sat down for a while thinking I was feeling like this because of the long flight, time difference etc but the nausea feeling would not go away.

As I looked around, I did not see any car hire kiosks, which is very odd in an airport arrival area. After a while I somehow found the energy to get up, even though it felt like I had concrete in my shoes, and wandered around to see if I could locate the well-known company who my car was booked with, but after no joy I found an information booth to see if they could help. All they could indicate to me, with very limited English, was to call the number on my booking form as 'no shop here'. I called the phone number attached to my paperwork and, of course, they only spoke Spanish so that conversation mainly consisted of me saying 'I only speak English' before they hung up. I went back to the information booth so they could translate and mediate the phone call, but they had now closed so I found a newsagent open and asked them if they could help me. They were very kind and phoned the car hire company on my behalf and subsequently advised me the company would call me back on my mobile when they had located an English-speaking operative. A few minutes later my mobile phone rang from the number I had previously called, but the person again only spoke Spanish. Over the next hour I spoke to 4 different operatives but none of them spoke English. Whilst still confused as to why there were no car hire places in the airport and feeling worn out, still with concrete shoes, I decided to just get a taxi to my hotel, which was quite close to the airport, and sort it out the following day.

During check in at the hotel a few things became apparent. The receptionist explained the reason I was feeling a bit 'strange' was probably due to altitude sickness, something that had not crossed my mind at all. She told me that Bogota is around 9000 feet above sea level and is one of the highest capital cities in the world, so it was quite normal to be feeling like I was and it 'should clear up in a few days when you get used to it'. I had never experienced altitude sickness anywhere in the world and it was a very bizarre feeling. It is probably not on anyone's checklist when booking a holiday or a trip abroad but checking the altitude above sea level is definitely now on my list of things to do!

I also discussed with the receptionist the car hire problem. She seemed amazed that I even wanted to hire a car, which puzzled me slightly, until she explained that the roads were not safe, there were lots of accidents and most people did not have insurance. Nearly everyone who was not local travelled around in taxis, hence why the demand at the airport for hire cars is virtually non-existent. She opened google maps on her phone and zoomed into Bogota centre and at that time (around 11.30pm) there were 45 live crashes! I still do this with friends now to explain the traffic issues in Bogota and I think the record is 68 crashes! I decided there and then, whilst under the influence of altitude sickness, I was not going to drive anywhere in South America. Of course, not all places in South America are unsafe to drive (there are a fair few though!) but it also reduced the stress of getting the car at the airport, driving and parking the car every day and then returning the car to the airport. I would have also had to do this twelve times as well, so the inner relief when I came to that decision was huge and a good one. It also transpired a far safer and cheaper one as well as taxis are very inexpensive, so it made sense for all concerned. After checking in I went straight to bed to try and clear my head of this weird feeling and luckily, I went out like a light.

The next morning I still felt a bit strange with the sickness but not as bad as when I landed. I called my company in the UK and advised them of the change to my hire car plans, got myself sorted and checked out of the hotel then got a taxi to the centre of Bogota which was going to be home for 3 days. The taxi picked me up and within a few miles I was celebrating my decision not to drive over there. It was totally lawless, like a scene from the wild west or the fairground 'bumper cars'. On the 20-minute or so journey to my hotel I saw 3 accidents in real time and about 7-8 on the roadside post-accident. It was like being on a Scalextric racetrack and everyone just seemed to have a total disregard for their own life. Apparently if you were involved in an accident you just sorted it out at the roadside with a pocket of cash and you were free to go for some more laps around the circuit. Now I fully understood why there was not a great demand for hire cars, and I was as happy as hell that I did not have one either.

My hotel was ok and in the middle of the banking business quarter, so quite modern with lots of little coffee shops and restaurants not far away. After partially unpacking I headed out to carry out my first audit in South America, which was a large modern hotel about a 10-minute walk away, which thankfully I completed without any problems and my initial impression of Colombian people was very good. I was made to feel welcome with friendly hospitality, good humour, courtesy and consideration, so I took it that these Colombians did not drive anywhere, and they must have got taxi's like everyone else.

After a quiet evening in the hotel and an early night, I woke up feeling a lot more normal (well, normal for me anyway). Reception booked my taxi to the first audit of the day, which was about

30 minutes' drive away, and as I got into the taxi, I went into tourist mode looking excitedly out of the window. There were some evidently very poor and run down areas of Bogota but what was becoming apparent was, apart from the hideous traffic and more real time accidents, was what seemed like a very large gathering of demonstrators all walking to a central point, which just so happened to be close my first audit of the day. I arrived at the audit hotel and as I got out of the taxi, I was met by two policeman who, I presume, wanted to know what I was doing there. Once they realised that I didn't speak Spanish they led me to the hotel where, once hotel security had unlocked the front door, a member of reception verified to them that I was ok to be there and that seemed to satisfy the police and they left. 'What the hell is going on' was ringing around my head at this point so once inside the hotel the hotel manager explained there were a lot of anti-government protests going on and in certain parts of the city they had imposed restrictions on free movement and if you didn't have a good reason to be in that area you were liable for arrest. During the audit it transpired the hotel had a major problem with the boiler flue, the exhaust from the boiler that removes the carbon monoxide gasses. The flue terminated about 1 metre from two bedrooms and with these windows open the gasses had the

potential to go into the room and literally gas the occupants to death. A similar problem in Corfu not so long ago did exactly that to two children whilst they were sleeping. The hotel manager, who was unaware of this risk, put the two bedrooms out of order and was frantically calling the boiler company to come and extend the flue to the top of the building. It also highlighted to me why the role of an auditor is of the utmost importance as it could literally save lives.

On that particular day it was reported that over 250,000 people were protesting in Bogota and the situation did escalate further over the following days with mass riots, curfews and even murders of police officers. This obviously changed my planned routine somewhat and the following days movements were literally my hotel, to the audit, to another audit, to my hotel. Going out after dark was 'not advised' and I did not need much persuasion to stay in my hotel. If I opened my bedroom window, all I could hear was helicopters hovering above and, in the distance, what sounded like gunfire and lots of shouting. It was a scary place to be.

The weather in Bogota was also very strange for a South American city, probably because of its altitude. One minute it was very cold and cloudy, next it was sunny and cold, then sunny and hot, then raining and hot, then raining and cold. That meant it was coat on, coat off, sun cream on and then coat back on, for most of the days I was there. It was also the last time I was going to need my coat for nearly 3 weeks.

Some of the people I came across in Bogota were some of the nicest people I have ever met. Parts of their city are beautiful with ultra-modern hotels with shops and restaurants dotted along the roadside. There are though, similar in lots of major cities, a lot of very poor areas very close by and of course within days of my arrival most of the city was under curfew as the rioting intensified. I felt sorry for them that my ill-timed trip unfortunately made my lasting memories of their city one of fear, rioting and of course the general chaos on their roads.

After a bite to eat in the hotel restaurant (where else could I go!) I had a very early night's sleep before my taxi picked me up at 2.30am for my early morning flight to Medellin.

Medellin

'Where are you flying to' asked the taxi driver on route to Bogota airport, 'Medellin' I replied, and he suddenly started laughing. Slightly confused I asked him what he was laughing at and it turned out it was my pronunciation that give him the giggles. I was saying it 'Med' 'el' 'lin', when apparently it should be pronounced 'Med' 'e' 'gin'. So after we had sorted that out and he had stopped laughing, he asked me where I was going to after Medellin. 'Cartagena' I told him, to an even louder fit of giggles from the driver before he eventually said 'No, no, no' and then carried on laughing. Apparently my 'Cart' 'a' 'gena' should have been 'Cart' 'a' 'hena'. So just to try and make sense of this, I needed to pronounce a double L as a G, and a G as an H? It might have been my lack of sleep, but this made no sense at all however from that moment on it was proudly pronounced correctly. I also found myself googling the other places I was due to visit to reduce the 'stupid tourist' effect!

Medellin is the birth, and resting place of Pablo Escobar, the Colombian drug lord and narco-terrorist who was the founder and sole leader of the Medellin Cartel. After escaping from prison in 1992, Escobar died 18 months later in 1993 after a shoot-out with the police, but by then he had amassed nearly 60 billion dollars (in today's money) from his cocaine business. Apparently, he hid a lot of this cash around Colombia in barrels and to this day there are still people looking for this hidden fortune. I began to wonder if Medellin was going to be a shrine to the 'great Escobar' who gave money and property to the poor, or had they seen fit to remove all traces of the murdering drug lord who destroyed families and had countless other victims. As I was only going to be in Medellin for less than 24 hours, with three audits to complete, it was unlikely I would find the time to explore this but I had hoped that I would get some sort of insight into the current feeling around the infamous local. I could always just go up to everyone I met and ask them 'hey, what did you think of that Pablo fellow?' but then again maybe that would not be such a good plan, so I decided against it....

The area between Bogota and Medellin is very mountainous so the views from the 5.30am flight were spectacular. As the sun was rising, you could see the snow-covered mountains with low level mist and cloud below, it was definitely something that was worth getting up at 2.30am to experience. The views from the airport to my hotel were also superb as Medellin is in a sort of bowl or hollow so as you followed the winding road down to the bottom, you were still above the early morning mist hovering over the city. It was an early but great start to the day.

I checked into to my hotel and they were kind enough to let me have breakfast and even though it was only 7.30am, I had been awake for 5 hours and it felt like lunch time! It was also started to get very warm as most of the early morning mist had now burned off to leave a clear blue sky. I arrived at my first audit around 10am but I had noticed during the taxi journey how modern the centre of Medellin appeared to be, the cars, the infrastructure, the buildings and now the hotel I had just arrived at, all seemed high quality. In the hot sunshine with clear skies and great views, it was a really nice place to be. The audit was fine, and the staff were also very accommodating throughout the hotel. I was sat around the pool, under an umbrella, typing up the report and enjoying whatever food and drink I wanted and I genuinely though at that point 'this is the best job in the world'. On any working trip abroad, you always experience some real low points, loneliness, homesickness etc but this was the flip side of that. It was perfect. I completed another 2 audits in the afternoon, and they were both as pleasant as the first, in similar high-quality establishments with great people. That evening I ventured out and found a lovely restaurant to end what had been the perfect day, albeit a very long one, and had another early night as the alarm was going off at 2.30am, again. I was waiting outside the hotel for my taxi to the airport at around 03.15am, It was so quiet and peaceful but still very warm and pleasant. The only sounds I could hear were the insects on their night shift when all of a sudden 'BOOOOM'! It sounded like a huge bomb had gone off not too far away and these were quickly followed by what sounded like rapid gunfire. I grabbed my case and rushed back into the hotel reception and shouted to the not so worried looking night manager 'did you hear that?' in a 'quick, hide!' kind of way. 'yes' he replied in a cool 'get a grip' kind of way, 'it is the demolition team blowing up the rocks to make way for a new hotel'. 'Why the hell are they doing it at 3.15 in the morning?' was the obvious question I asked, to which he replied, 'it would alarm too many people if they did it during the day'. Oh that's alright then, I thought, just wake everyone up thinking they are been invaded. It seemed barmy logic to me but maybe when Pablo Escobar was operating in these parts, the sounds of bombs going off had a whole different meaning and perspective.

As I was waiting in the departure lounge of Medellin airport, I realised that I had not seen anything relating to Pablo Escobar anywhere. It was not like I was expecting market sellers to be shouting 'get your Pablo t-shirts here' and offering all sorts of memorabilia but there was nothing and I imagined the Medellin government had deliberately tried to remove all trace of him. Pablo was gone, but his victims and families still had to live with what he had done, and that is totally understandable.

I was only in Medellin for less than 24 hours, but I loved it and would not hesitate to go back there if I ever got the chance.

Cartagena

My destination today was Cartagena, a major shipping port in the north of Colombia on the Caribbean coast. After flying from Medellin back to Bogota airport, then onto Cartagena I had a similar days plan to the one in Medellin, 3 audits followed by an early night, followed by another early morning the next day so in truth I did not get to see a great deal of the city. The parts I did see were ok, but it very busy everywhere and even on a short taxi journey you spent most of the time just sat in traffic.

The first 2 hotels I inspected were in the centre of Cartagena and these were old, small properties that did not exactly come up to standard. If a hotel is higher than 3 floors and all enclosed (internal corridors etc) within the building, there is a requirement to have two separate fire escapes, so you always have another way to evacuate in case of a fire. Both of these hotels only had one way out, as well as no way to control the spread of smoke either. If a fire started on the ground floor, the only place the flames and smoke could go was up the one flight of open stairs and into every corridor. If you're on the fifth floor you then had the impossible job of coming down a smoke and fire filled staircase to escape, which gives you zero percent chance of making it before you would be overcome with smoke. The hotels required major refurbishment to accommodate another 'protected from smoke' staircase which would mean removing about 14 bedrooms. For the time being my recommendation was only to use the ground floor until they could resolve the problem. If you have ever requested a high floor in a hotel but were given a very low floor, there may be another reason for it.

The last audit of the day being a fantastic modern beach fronted complex, but they refused to let me carry out the inspection as they were unaware of it and asked me to leave! Apparently, this was a mistake by someone in an office, somewhere, but it did mean I had a few hours off to go for a good long walk down the beach front and have a few beers in the sun, which was nice. After an awful meal in my hotel, with a beef burger sent back to the chef 3 times because it was so undercooked it was still mooing, I settled down for another early night. At this point I also noticed my left hand was becoming a bit itchy but thought nothing more about it and went to sleep.

After a fairly unsettled few hours' sleep, my alarm went off at 3am and I noticed my left hand was by now bloody sore. I had evidently been bitten by mosquito's, once just by the bottom of my nail on my little finger and once on the knuckle of my thumb. I had 2 massive, painful lumps that were so itchy I could have rubbed them with a cheese-grater, and every time I moved my hand this feeling intensified. Maybe at 3am in Medellin whilst waiting for my taxi, the night shift insects wanted to give me something to remember them by. Bastards. It took about a week for these bites to go and everywhere I went in that time people always looked, pointed, and said 'ooh, that looks painful'. No shit.

I arrived at Cartagena airport at about 4.30am for my flight to my next location, San Andres and to be honest I wasn't in the greatest of moods. I was tired and cranky, and my left hand looked and felt like it had a major disease so as I approached airport security I had hoped for no issues. As I have travelled the world for business or leisure, airport security continues to baffle me. Not the requirement for it as this I fully understand, it is the general public and the inconsistencies of what is required that never ceases to amaze me. There are signs everywhere telling you what you can and cannot take through, sometimes accompanied by recorded messages played over the speakers, to inform you what you need to do i.e. belt and shoes off, clear bag with all liquids inside etc. Now I do not know if it is because the majority of people are already in holiday mode or just generally stupid, but common sense goes out of the window and their ability to read or listen also disappears. Then add to this the fact that the requirements change from country to country. Some airports want everything in one bag, some want everything out of the bag, some want certain things in, certain things out, belts and shoes on, belts and shoes off etc. and this is why there are always waiting times to get through security. If we are clever enough to put a man on the moon, surely, we have the capability to improve this procedure without jeopardising security? Granted though, stupid people will always be stupid.

I have gone through airport security hundreds of times with no issues but this time it would be very different. I stopped smoking about 8 years ago and I have been vaping ever since. Why I have replaced the need for tobacco with strawberry milkshake flavoured vape may seem a bit strange, but it does stop me from wanting to smoke and that is surely a good thing? It is, until you pass through Cartagena airport with them. I have always followed the rules with regards to how much liquid I can take through as hand luggage and as the batteries have to be carried on, these are also in my carry-on bag. I have done this through every airport and not once has there been any problems. After taking off my belt, shoes etc I placed my bag on the conveyor belt and went through the scanner. All good so far. I then notice that my bag had taken a side belt to where a rather unhappy looking security lady was waiting for it, again, this has happened before and is quite normal as they want to check what has shown up on the screen. She looked inside my bag and said something in Spanish to which I replied, 'do you speak English'? Evidently, she did not as she continued in Spanish so I indicated to my phone so I could translate through the app but that was a definite 'no', as she pointed to a picture sign indicating 'no phones in this area'. She then removed my 2 vape batteries and the small amount of liquid (2 x 10ml) and placed them on the table in front of her and said 'no'. I looked at her and said' what do you mean, 'no'? She rambled away in Spanish again but I did clearly understand the word 'no' and something that sounded like 'confiscate' so I began to tell her that I was allowed to take these through, as per the rules, and could not understand what the problem was, when she was joined by a stocky male security operative and they began a conversation, which again resulted in a 'no'. I was now getting madder by the second and was, without trying to be awkward, raising my voice in frustration. I motioned to get at my phone again but again the picture sign was pointed out to me. I was again explaining it was only vaping equipment, whilst ridiculously doing the vaping action, when the stocky guy clearly said 'confiscate'.

What followed, I can only apologise for as I appreciate, they were only doing their jobs. I told them both to 'fuck off', loudly and this obviously created a bit of a scene in a busy security area, but then they started shouting back, loudly, which only riled me even more. It escalated fairly quickly and at this stage I was in the face of the stocky guy telling him exactly what I thought about him, his choice of after-shave, his hairstyle, shoe size and anything else I could muster together in my head. We were then joined by 2 policemen, with guns, who tried to calm the situation down. The 4 of them then had a chat, which again resulted in a 'no' and 'confiscate', so they were told to 'fuck off' as well. At that particular point I had lost it and did not really care what the consequences were going to be. They had stopped anyone else coming through security so they could deal with this deranged English guy, which obviously resulted in a large queue the other side. I was then ushered into a side room along with my bag and vaping equipment, my 2 security operatives and the 2 policemen, with guns. The stocky security guy had brought with him a sort of 'confiscation' box and subsequently started to pick up my vape and put them into this box when I swotted his arm away and told him to 'get your fucking hands off my stuff'. We now had a Colombian standoff and the policemen started to look trigger happy. To lighten the mood I shouted to all 4 of them 'you can all fuck off, I am taking these through security and not one of you are going to fucking stop me' and then promptly yelled at them all to 'fuck off' again. They all began talking to each other again and then bizarrely, without indicating anything further to me, all left the room. I stood there for about 5 minutes waiting for the next stage of 'no', but no one came back. I calmly placed everything back into my bag and walked out into the departure lounge where five hundred fellow passengers refused any sort of eye contact whilst all probably thinking 'another stupid person'.

It was surreal and I sat there wondering what the hell had just happened. I had followed the rules by not packing batteries in my hold luggage and only had 20ml of liquid with me in total. Vaping was not illegal in Colombia and I had also gone through 4 airport security's in the same country, with the same equipment, with no issues. Why the security and the police reacted the way they did was probably down to lack of knowledge or training, possibly? My reaction was probably down to the language barrier, lack of sleep, stress and the knowledge that if they had of confiscated my vaping equipment, I would have been on 40 cigarettes a day for evermore. How I got away with reacting like I did though, I will never know, and I am still surprised that I did not wake up the next day in a Colombian prison. Even though they probably had no idea what I was yelling at them, they probably gathered I was not inviting them for afternoon tea because I loved them all.

I was explaining this incident to a hotelier in San Andres when he told me that the security operatives probably wanted a bribe off me to take the vape through and when they realised that this wasn't going to happen, and with the scene it was creating, they had no choice but to let me through with them. I have no idea if this is correct though and at no point was any of this indicated to me during the incident. It would not have been a good idea for me to have tried to bribe them either if that is not what they had wanted!

After calming down and paying my 'tourist tax' I boarded my aircraft for the hour and a half flight to San Andres for a 1-night stay, to complete just 2 audits.

San Andres

San Andres is a tiny island in the Caribbean Sea, which even though it is Colombian, is actually closer to Nicaragua and Jamaica than it is to

Colombia. It also has some rich history with the UK and to this day the English language is still spoken by many, which was obviously a great relief to me!

After passing through the arrival lounge, I caught a taxi to my hotel, which I was not looking forward to. It was in fact a hostel and that conjured all sorts of images in my head of 16 people to a room, on bunk beds, with a bucket in the corner for the shared toilet. I could not have been more wrong. It was fantastic, clean and probably the biggest room, bar Las Vegas, that I have ever stayed in. It had all the mod con's with satellite TV, air conditioning and thankfully my own bathroom!

I was beginning to unpack when I suddenly realised I had about 15 minutes before my first audit, which was about 20 minutes' walk away on the pedestrianised sea front, so I collected my laptop etc and headed out. The views in San Andres are stunning and is sort of how you imagine paradise looks like. Palm trees, blue sky, white sand and perfect waves crashing ashore and it was about 40 degrees. If you were here on holiday this must have been the absolute perfect day, but I was fully dressed, carrying a heavy man bag and was late. I walked as fast as I could, bought some water, walked some more, then bought some more water but by now I was soaked to the skin in sweat and as I also suffer from hay fever, the palm trees were playing havoc with my eyes and I also started sneezing continually. I eventually walked into the reception of the hotel I was auditing looking like I had just been for a swim, whilst suffering with flu. I must have looked horrendous as the first thing the receptionist did was call housekeeping to bring me some towels and then the bar to bring me some water! After drying off and cooling down in the air conditioning I completed the audit with the only problem being the height of the balconies that were too low and I was on to the next audit, which luckily was just around the corner so I arrived there looking a lot more normal and completed the inspection but again the height of the balconies were an issue. Ideally a balcony height should be 1.1 metre or higher, a height of 1 metre is allowed albeit with a recommendation to extend to 1.1 metre but anything less than 1 metre has a potential to cause someone to inadvertently fall over it or climb over it. In both these hotels the recommendation was for no children under the age of 14 to be accommodated in rooms with a balcony until they had sorted the problem out. It was now around 2pm and my work in San Andres was complete, but I was not getting my flight out until 6pm the following day so I planned to enjoy as much of this paradise island whilst I had the chance. I went back to my hostel, unpacked and changed into something more appropriate and headed to the beach for a few hours. It was bliss and the only thing missing to make it absolutely perfect, was my wife. So I called her and told her how fantastic it was and whilst she was in cold, wet and windy England I am sure she really appreciated that! That evening I headed back out to the bars and restaurants on the sea front, it was just like being on holiday to a dream destination and it was still very hot. After drinking far too much and staggering back to the hostel I settled down to sleep in the knowledge I had no alarm set, which was a wonderful feeling after the recent early mornings I had just had. After a leisurely morning, one last long walk down the lovely sea front, more sunbathing and a spot of late lunch it was time to head back to the airport to catch a flight to Bogota, then straight onto a flight to Quito, Ecuador. I arrived at the airport about 3 hours before departure and could not wait to get through to the departure lounge to sit in the air conditioning as apart from it being very hot, and I was also wearing jeans, I was now also turning into a shade of lobster red. Inside the lounge it wasn't as cool as I had hoped for, then there was a power cut. After a few minutes, the power was back on and it was just starting to cool down again when there was another power cut. As it turned out, the air conditioning system was the cause of the power cuts, so the airport staff had obviously decided to turn the air conditioning off. Like most airport departure lounges they are glass fronted with views over the runway but with the 40-degree heat outside, this small lounge was in effect turning into a greenhouse. It was unbearable but then the bad news really started to flow in as there was an announcement over the speakers in Spanish which made everyone instantly unhappy. I went up to the departure desk to ask what the information was, but the airline rep didn't speak English so I was in the process of getting my translate app in action when I was approached by a very helpful guy who did speak English and he told me the bad news. Our flight to Bogota had been delayed by at least 4 hours. Now I had already been in the departure lounge about 2 hours and I was already sweating profusely so the thought of sitting in it for a further 5 hours did not help my mood one little bit. This was also going to cause another major problem; I was going to miss my connecting flight to Quito and therefore not make it to my hotel there either and this could cause the domino effect I was concerned about before I went on the trip. When you are calm, cool and composed you can deal with most things that life throws at you, but when you are hot, stressed and cannot communicate with people it makes this type of scenario very difficult to deal with and by definition you react differently. Imagine playing chess in a sauna whilst fully dressed, are you going to be thinking clearly? The main reason I was going into panic mode was down to the heat, no question, and ultimately, if I missed flights through no fault of my own, I would just normally go with the flow and did not worry about it, but the heat was having a strange effect on me and I was struggling to think clearly. My company had a 24-help line for auditors all around the world to use in case of emergency so I decided to call them so they could try to rearrange plans, avoid no-show costs etc. Nobody answered. I must have called 10 times, but nobody picked up and I was getting more and more agitated. I called my wife and she even tried the 24-hour number, but she got the same response I did, which was none. I even tried some of my colleagues in the UK office but due to the time difference, it was the middle of the night in the UK so understandably they did not respond. I then emailed certain people regarding my predicament so at least when they got into the office, they would be aware of it and maybe they could put a plan B into action.

The role of an auditor doing this type of job is by definition a lonely and isolated one, but this is the first time that I properly felt alone and helpless.

Every time there was an airline announcement, my English speaking friend would come over to me and let me know what had been said, the latest being the airline would sort out overnight accommodation for us once we landed in Bogota as we were going to miss our respective connecting flights. The one positive was it was the same airline for both flights so it was their responsibility to accommodate me, or that would have been more hassle to arrange. We were also given a sort of 'packed lunch' off the airline which in that heat was barely edible, but the drink was appreciated. From walking into the departure lounge to eventually boarding the aircraft was the longest 7 hours of my life, and I also never received a call back from the 24-hour helpline.

After landing in Bogota my English-speaking friend never left my side as instructions of what to do next were constantly being translated. We queued up for our hotel voucher and we were told the new connecting flight to Quito would be tomorrow evening, which was absolutely no use to me as I was only going to be in Quito to carry out 1 audit in the afternoon before flying onto Peru, so I asked my new friend to enquire on my behalf regarding getting my case offloaded. My friend took me through the airport to the correct office, spoke to them on my behalf and arranged with them to get my case brought to me, the only snag being this process could take up to 2 hours, but I had no other choice. Without the help of my English-speaking friend, who incidentally came from Brazil, I would have been in an even bigger mess than I was already in and I could not thank him enough. He was genuinely just a good human being and I am eternally grateful for the help he gave me that evening. After waiting for an hour and a half my case finally appeared but as I had missed the free shuttle bus to the airline arranged hotel, I got a taxi. It was now 2am and what had started out as the perfect day in San Andres had now ended with uncertainty and stress as I also needed to be up early because I had no idea what rearranged flight etc I was going to be on. I set the alarm for 7am and it was a good job I did as it turned out I was going to be on a 11.45 flight to Quito, so after a quick shower and breakfast I headed back to the Bogota airport. After a discussion with the UK office regarding their ever so helpful 24hour helpline, it transpired they had given me the wrong number which they were very apologetic over and subsequently gave me the correct number just in case I needed it. Whoever owned the number I was calling must have wondered what the hell was going on when they listened to their voicemails though!

Whilst waiting in the queue for the check in at the airport, I started a conversation with a young

American girl in front of me. She was backpacking around the world, alone, before she went back to college in the United States. She had already visited some of the places I was due to go to, so it was a pleasant and informative chat that also helped pass the time as the queue seemed to be stuck in glue. When I told her what I was doing in South America, she replied 'wow, that has got to be the best job in the world' and to be honest it should be. A former colleague of mine once said something similar but ended it with 'but something always fuck's it up', and the last 12 or so hours paid testament to that.

Chapter 2

Ecuador

Quito, the capital of Ecuador, is the 2nd highest capital city in the world and the one closest to the equator. According to my American backpacker, it is also a lovely place to visit and hence why she was going back there again on her way home. I was not going to be seeing any of it though, apart from the airport and 1 hotel, as I was flying back out that evening to Peru.

I subsequently landed and instantly felt a little queasy due to the altitude but as I had experienced this in Bogota when I had landed there, I managed to ignore it. My taxi driver was explaining to me that Quito was unique as it is so high (9000 feet above sea level) even Malaria could not survive. I was mightily impressed by this until I googled it whilst waiting for the hotel manager to join me. Malaria cannot survive at anything over 5000 feet, so it was not 'that' unique and I suppose as none of the locals were ever going to get the disease, it did seem a bit irrelevant. It's like me telling everyone that you have no chance of dying in Liverpool from lava from a local volcano, because there are no bloody volcanoes there! Considering that Quito is surrounded by volcanoes, I am surprised he didn't mention that fact to me so I could prepare myself for all that lava that was going to burn me alive, but no, I won't catch Malaria whilst in Quito. Thanks for that.

The hotel I was inspecting was not that far from the very busy airport and I subsequently completed the audit, which was just about ok apart from some issues with fire testing (they weren't!) and staff training (they hadn't), and returned to check in for my next flight to Lima, the capital of Peru.

Chapter 3

Peru

Peru

'Try and get me something about Paddington Bear whilst you are in Peru' was the request from my wife before I left home. As Paddington comes from 'darkest Peru' it must have conjured up images of shop after shop full of Paddington memorabilia that could have filled my case up. So, full of promises, I confirmed I would keep my eye out for her.

Lima

The 2.5-hour flight started a little curiously, as most of the passengers started praying and what sounded like the reciting of a hymn. There was one guy doing 'a reading', then everyone else joined in for the chorus at the end of each line. It was nice in one way as I had not seen anything like this, but it did worry me slightly that they knew something that I did not regarding this flight.
The couple in my row of three seats then started chatting away in Spanish so I had no idea what they are saying, but the lady next to me then proceeded to get the largest laptop I have ever see out of her bag and starts it up. Then she play's a video, which was a close up of a baby

having a cleft lip operation. Now I am a little squeamish with this type of thing, but didn't want to say anything as it could be their baby, or she could be a surgeon brushing up on her skills and no doubt will offend if I would have asked her to turn it off. Is it ok to play that type of video/ operation on a plane? I am not so sure, but I spent 2 hours looking out of the window at darkness. For 2 days, if I turned my head to the right it felt like I had whiplash.

I arrived in Lima and made my way through to the arrival lounge looking for a mobile/ sim kiosk, but they were all shut so the plan was to get one the next day as I was only heading straight to the hotel for sleep and wouldn't need phone data anyway as when I got to the hotel, with Wi-Fi, I could message home etc.

The only way to describe outside Lima airport is by comparing it to Finding Nemo. Think of the hundreds of seagulls saying 'mine, mine, mine' whilst chasing the fish in the harbour but replace the seagulls for taxi drivers saying 'taxi, taxi, taxi'. There are also massive signs up indicating shouting 'taxi' is an offence, but no one seemed to take any notice.

After ignoring all the seagulls, I got into the taxi rank queue with my hotel name and address ready on my phone screen and eventually arrived at the front of the queue. The next taxi pulled up, and I presumed in Spanish, asked where I want to go, so I showed him my prepared phone, he looked at the details and shouted 'No' and then beckoned the person behind me forward. Slightly bemused I waited for the next taxi to arrive and exactly the same happened! I was then approached by a taxi driver (one of the seagulls) who asked in relatively good English where I wanted to go to, so I showed him. 'No problem, 270 Sol'. When I landed, I got some currency but that in my mind was expensive (turned out to be about £70!) so politely said no and decided to go back into the terminal where I found a policeman. He spoke virtually no English but enough to tell me that the area that my hotel was located in was 'very dangerous', hence why the first 2 taxis had refused to take me. It was now about 11.30pm and I had been awake for nearly 17 hours, including 2 flights and the work completed in Ecuador. I went outside to vape and think and noticed the on-site airport hotel directly opposite, so I went over to the hotel reception to try and book a room, but the hotel was fully booked. I am walking back to the arrival lounge when the 270 Sol taxi driver comes back over to me. Bear in mind he has a suit on, a lanyard with his photo on and he is happy to take me to the hotel when no one else will, I have no internet so cannot book somewhere else, nothing is open in the terminal and I desperately need sleep. I was thinking that even if it is terrible I can cope for 1 night and sort it out the next day when I had internet and had managed to get some sleep and I also couldn't stay in the airport terminal so I decided, reluctantly, to agree for him to take me albeit for a slightly reduced 250 Sol. We got into his taxi, which was just a private car with no meter (quite normal) and he asked for payment upfront, again nothing too strange as this has happened on this trip before. He drove for about 10 minutes and stops and points to a derelict run-down building, and says, 'your hotel'. He tells me to wait in the car whilst he went to find the exact building it was in, so he locked the doors and wandered off. Withing seconds there was a gang of youths walking around the car, shouting, laughing, and banging on the bonnet. I heard the driver shouting at them and they all ran off whilst I presume hurling abuse to him as they dispersed. There was no way I was even getting out of the car in this area let alone walk around with my laptop etc, so the driver says, 'not safe here, I know a better hotel with security'. Now I did notice during the journey not far from the airport a Holiday Inn, so I asked him to take me there to which he replied 'unfortunately the Holiday Inn is full, I took a guest there before and they have no rooms left'. Without internet I could not check either. So I agreed to go to the 'better hotel'. We arrived in an area that had no street lighting, so it was very dark apart from a run-down hotel and the driver got out of the car and beckoned me in. It was more akin to a rundown back-street bed and breakfast but again I thought as long as the room is secure and clean, I could cope with 1 night here so followed him in.

After my driver and the receptionist had exchanged words, the guy behind the counter said '$100 a night', but I told them I wanted to see the accommodation first, so we all went upstairs to see the room. It was a flea pit, the A/C unit had been removed leaving a clear hole in the wall to outside and the smell was horrendous. I told the taxi driver I was not staying here and was heading back to reception when the hotel 'receptionist' said '$50 a night' to which I replied, 'I am not staying here' and walked out of the building, so the taxi driver opened the car and we got in. I told him to take me to the Holiday Inn as at least they would have Wi-Fi and I could sort something from there and even though he said it was full he seemed to agree that he would take me. He briefly spoke with the receptionist through the car window and after unnecessarily waiting for a few minutes off we went.

He drove a few hundred yards and stopped in complete darkness. He turns the inside light on, turns to me and says he wants another 250 Sol to take me to the Holiday Inn. I tell him that he has already ripped me off and he has had plenty to cover the brief journeys....when I became aware that the car is surrounded by 4-5 men in dark clothing with their hoods up....he repeated his demands in a far more angry tone and I repeated my response which by now was also in an angry tone...he in turn communicated with the external gang outside when suddenly, through the window next to me I can see a gun, similar to a Browning 9mm, tapping the barrel on the glass....he repeats his demands and I told him I will pay him what he wants when we get to the Holiday inn but he wanted the money 'NOW' in a much more aggressive tone. I tell him to take me and I will pay him when we get there. At this stage I am ready for whatever is coming my way as I am so tired and mad, I am starting to lose my cool, which in this situation is not a good mix. The men outside now start shouting at me through the glass window, whilst now making it very clear that they have guns by repeatedly tapping the glass. I tell the driver to 'fuck off' whilst repeating that I will pay him more money if he takes me to the Holiday Inn. I am now shaking with anger and fear. He says something to the gang outside and suddenly they move away, and we are driving again, and within in a few miles of total silence he pulls up outside the Holiday inn. He demands the money again and I tell him to open my door (child locks are on) and to get my case out. He says he wants his money before he will let me out, so I started banging on the window to get the attention of the Holiday inn security until he opens my door and gets my case. He holds his hand out for the money, I reached towards him and tell him to 'fuck off' right into his face and suddenly he did not appear to be that brave anymore, so I walked towards the entrance without paying him a penny more. I was telling the Holiday inn security what had just happened when the taxi driver sped away. I went inside to reception, shaking, and asked if they had any vacant rooms, 'yes, we have loads' was the reply.

I booked in, opened my bedroom door, pushed my case in the room and headed straight down to the bar that they were going to keep open for me. I made full use of that bar until about 3am and I was not tired anymore.

Now I am well-travelled, never put myself in a bad situation, follow the travel advice etc, so how the hell did I end up in that situation? I put it down to a list of factors such as late flight arrival, no sleep, no sim card/ internet, piss poor hotel choice by my company (the location of the hotel is indeed listed as 'dangerous' on the government website) and a well organised scum bag. Lessons were learnt all round that night by the company that sent me and certainly by me and even as I am writing this my heart rate is going through the roof because it was bloody scary.

Incidentally, a week after my incident, 2 guys were shot dead as they got out of an airport taxi at their hotel in Buenos Aires, Argentina. A sobering thought.

Next morning, after various high-level conversations with some of the Directors of the company who had sent me over there and lots of apologies and with lessons learnt by all concerned, I was booked into another hotel in the centre of Lima old town to complete some more audits. I arranged for the Holiday Inn to get me a taxi to my next hotel but asked the driver to drive past my original hotel from the night before so I could see it in daylight. It was a slum and did not even resemble accommodation.

I arrived and was pleasantly surprised by my new hotel. It was not fantastic by any stretch, but it was modern, clean and had everything I needed whilst I was staying there. I checked in and completed the afternoon audit with no issues, and as it was only 100 yards from my hotel no taxi was required! Next day I only had 1 audit to do and it was about a mile away around lunch time, so again I decided to walk. I underestimated just how hot it was though and by the time I got there I was soaked in sweat and slightly confused as there was not a sign for the company I was looking for, even though I was at the right address. It transpired they had moved 2 years ago much to my dismay and even the building security guys did not know where they had moved to. Perfect. You would have thought that the UK office would at least check that they are sending auditors to addresses and companies that actually existed? Now just another long hot walk back to my hotel, and the bar.

Cusco

The next day I was flying to Cusco after one early morning audit in Miraflores, about a 20-minute taxi ride from my hotel. After checking out of my hotel my booked taxi arrived and we set off, with a total non-English speaking driver. As with most South American countries, driving anywhere is an experience. The roads were always log jammed, in terrible condition (Uruguay apart) and even the locals say you have to be crazy to drive there. After about 10 minutes we were sat in 4 lanes of stationary traffic, whilst everyone's favourite pass time of pressing their vehicles horn is in full flow.
Suddenly I noticed smoke coming into the vehicle from the vents at the front. The driver mutters something and gets out of the car and heads to the boot, whilst he has already motioned me to stay put. He reappears with a fire extinguisher and lifts the bonnet on the car, whilst returning

to me and again indicated to stay where I was. This did not sit too well with me as the car was now filling up with smoke! Suddenly a policewoman appeared at my window and whilst I was trying to open the door, she closed it again and puts her hand up in a 'stay' kind of way. I shouted, 'the fucking car is on fire, let me out', but the hand returned, and I therefore stayed put. The driver in the meantime is emptying his extinguisher over the engine until flames could not be seen anymore. At last, the policewomen opened my door, but only after her colleagues had stopped the non- existent flow of traffic to allow me to push my suitcase through a wall of horn noise and vehicles to the hard shoulder. The taxi was eventually also pushed onto the hard shoulder. The Policewoman did not speak any English (which was by now expected), so I was stood there with my suitcase, the taxi driver and the police, wondering how this was going to play out. After about 30 minutes another taxi appeared, and the 'hand' indicated I was to get in. I arrived a little late for my audit, but in one piece. Directly opposite the hotel was an Irish bar, with an advert saying they sold 'real Guinness' (in relation to 'pretend Guinness'?), but it was 10am in the morning and they did not open until 5pm much to my dismay.....still no Guinness!. My flight to Cusco was at 6pm so after completing the audit I headed to the airport about 3pm, checked in and got some food.

Cusco is over 11000 feet above sea level which can cause sever altitude sickness if you are not used to it. Bogota is around 9000 feet above sea level and that impacted me in a big way, so I read up on all the advice of how to combat the effects before I arrived in Cusco. These included taking it easy (yeah right), acclimatising for a few days (I had 4 planned audits in my 2 days there), avoiding alcohol (I will try but can't promise....) and drinking lot of water (no problem as I was a sweaty mess most of the time anyway). Other advice was to take some altitude sweets, which you could buy in the airport chemist, and drinking coca cola (other brands are apparently just as effective).

I found the coco sweets on 'a buy 2 get the 3rd free' offer in the airport chemist so bought 3 packs without a second thought and asked the pharmacist how many I should be taking to nullify the effects of altitude sickness to which she replied 'have a few before you take off, then a few on the plane, then a few each day and you should be fine'. Perfect, I have just bought enough to keep me going for about 3 weeks, but I am only there for 2 days, but undeterred I start munching away. Not a great taste, a mix of cheap chocolate and soft caramel that took the lining off the roof of my mouth, but if they worked it would be worth it and I was washing it down with diet coke for the added benefits. The flight, about 2.5 hours, was delayed an hour because of bad weather, so more coco sweets and diet coke until we finally boarded and took off. The flight was a little bumpy but with more diet coke from the trolley and a few more coco sweets I was ready to take on this altitude problem head on. We then flew into a severe thunderstorm and I imagine if you are stuck inside a child's rattle it must feel exactly like I did on this flight. People were praying, screaming and shouting in fear and all I could do to make me feel better was to have more coco sweets. Then there was an announcement from the captain that were in the middle of some bad weather (no shit) and he was going to circle above it until they could land. For 1 hour we circled, so more diet coke and more coco sweets (now on the 2nd pack) and the captain stated he was going to attempt to land. It was horrendous. Lightning, gale force winds, lashing rain and we were back inside the child's rattle. He eventually aborted and stated he was going back to Lima, so then we had another 2.5 hours back to where we come from to make it the 6-hour flight to nowhere.

I then had 2 problems. The first, and totally out of my control, was the following days audits would have to be cancelled unless I could get on an early flight the next day, but I could only sort that out when I landed to see what the options were.

The 2nd problem, and much more pressing than the first, was I had drunk that much diet coke (caffeine) and ate so many coco sweets (caffeine) I was virtually bouncing off the walls. If I could have gone for a run it would have outdone Forest Gump, I had that much energy I had developed muscle Tourette's. When we landed back in Lima, I could not think straight at all, whilst everyone else seemed glad they were alive after the flight, I was walking around the luggage carousel in a 'wired' daze until I spotted my suitcase, 3 carousels away going around and around on its own.

We had to go back to the check in desk and queue up to rebook, but it was apparent the next available flight to Cusco was 3 days away as all flights had been cancelled for 24 hours and alternative flights had been rebooked very quickly. It was now midnight and I had no hotel as I should have been in Cusco, so I thought I would call the 24-hour helpline in the UK as this should now work after the previous incident.

'Do you know what time it is?' came the reply from the girl I had evidently awoken from a coma, 'its 5am' she said before I had chance to check my worldwide clock. I explained my problem and she replied' do what you need to do' and hung up. I hope she never gets a job at the Samaritans or the suicide rate will rocket. I manage to book into the on-site airport hotel, for 2 nights and headed for the bar, but at 4am I was still wide awake and still felt the need to jog on the spot.

I woke up at midday, with a hangover from hell, to a raft of missed calls, emails and rebooked flights, but I was basically staying in Lima airport until the following morning before catching a flight to Montevideo, Uruguay. That afternoon, after heading into the airport for some food, I went to the hotel bar where I started a conversation with the barman, who spoke really good English. He used to work on cruise ships all over the world and it was really nice to have a face to face chat with someone and especially where we both understood each other without any need for the translate app. That was until I asked him if he sold Guinness, 'no, but we do sell something very similar' so I excitedly ordered one. No, it was not similar at all, it was dark in colour and that was it. In fact it tasted like cider that had gone bad, so I went back on the local Peru lager to try and get rid of the taste. I was tempted, after a few beers, to go for a walk around the airport arrival lounge to see if I could find my taxi scumbag, just so I could have a nice little chat with him, but I decided against it. In Peru, I didn't have to look for trouble as it seemed to find me no problem anyway, but I do wish I had found him, had 'a chat' with him and then point him out to the police but who would have believed me anyway and what proof did I have?

After a few more local beers I was heading to bed for an early night ahead of another early start the next day.

My lasting memory of Peru is obviously not a good one as, like most things in life, it comes down to personal experience and your own expectations. You can see the difference on trip advisor reviews regarding a certain hotel, anywhere in the world, on the same week can vary dramatically. 'the food was fantastic' or 'the food was terrible', or 'the staff were brilliant' compared to 'the staff were awful' for the exactly the same hotel sums that up, it depends on what you expected and what you ended up with. There are probably lots of people who visit Peru and think it is fantastic, but they obviously had a different experience to me.

If your trip had been organised properly, you only used pre-booked taxi's, you stayed in good hotels in good areas and you can speak Spanish, I imagine your impression of Peru would be totally different to mine.

I think I must have seen 'darkest Peru', but I did not see a single thing relating to Paddington bear anywhere.

Chapter 4

Uruguay

Uruguay

Uruguay is the second most expensive country in South America, after Chile. Incidentally, I was due to spend about a week in Chile and Easter island, but it got cancelled at the last minute because of major civil unrest in the capital, Santiago, so it was quite rightly decided that it was not worth the risk sending me there. I can get into enough trouble on my own thanks, but I was still disappointed I wasn't going to visit there.

Montevideo

Montevideo was like a breath of fresh air, not that it was any cooler temperature wise than anywhere else, but it felt different. All the cars were in good condition, the road network looked brand new and the roads were generally quiet, it was also a lot more laid back and clean. It just felt 'nice'. All the people I met there were pleasant and helpful and most had a fairly good understanding of the English language, reason being (I was told) is that a lot of the students go to college in America to learn, then return to Uruguay to live and work.

My first hotel was in the business district and it was awful. The lift had a step of about a foot to get in and out, the room was tiny, the air conditioning unit sounded like a generator and did not really cool anything but more importantly the hotel had no fire alarm and I was on the 8th floor. So after a very unpleasant night's sleep, and a further call to the UK company, I checked out and found a lovely hotel facing the beach where I stayed for my short stay in Uruguay.

My first days auditing went without a hitch and the hoteliers seemed happy for me to be there, the standards were very good, and they also had a genuine interest to improve what was lacking. You are normally greeted on arrival by one of the hotel managers who escorts you around the property and then generally cannot wait to see the back of you, but after arriving at one particular property I was escorted into the boardroom and there sat to attention was the head chef, head housekeeper, reception manager, maintenance manager along with director of the hotel! It was like walking into an interview but they were all really nice and even after the audit we all met up again so they could hear my feedback on every department. It was a refreshing change to the normal and enhanced the 'nice' feelings I had towards Montevideo.

It was now Friday night and I had two days off, i.e. no flying or audits, in fact they were my only days off in the 3 weeks I spent in South America so on the Saturday I went exploring the local area.

The beach in Montevideo is fantastic, but virtually empty as it is not exactly a holiday destination, so it is only used by a few locals. This may be the just time of year I was there (December) but it was their summer season and it seemed a bit strange as it was 36 degrees without a cloud in the sky. I wandered out to the seafront and settled in at the beach bar for a few beers in the sun and it felt like paradise. After a further walk I found a Hard Rock Café and had a lovely late lunch by the harbour before finding a modern shopping centre that was quite busy with Christmas shoppers, but I was more interested in the air conditioning! I googled 'Irish bar near to me' and low and behold there was one on the way back to the hotel. It was shut but opened at 6pm so that was my evening planned. It was only when I got back to my hotel when I realised with my 'step' app that I had walked nearly 6 miles! I did go back to the Irish bar later on, but they had never heard of Guinness and I doubt any of the staff even knew where Ireland was on a map, but it was pleasant, and the food was good. In the small talk with the staff the obvious 'where are you from' question was asked and again it ended with 'ah Mo Salah' which is a little odd, as with his recent history with Liverpool FC surely their former forward Luiz Suarez (now at Barcelona) being from Uruguay would more likely get mentioned? But no it was still Mo Salah. It also felt very safe walking back to the hotel along the sea front as it approached midnight.

Next day I repeated most of what I did Saturday, minus the shopping centre, but did include Hard Rock again and had a bonus paddle in the sea. I also found a coffee shop/ bookstore on the sea front that had the world's best (apparently) cakes and to be fair I could not argue. The strawberry gateaux I had was superb.

I only had 1 audit on the Monday which was at 11am and a 20 minute walk away, so I planned another afternoon around the beach but when I arrived the manager asked if I could come back at 2pm as he was busy so that was that plan shot to bits. He probably wasn't busy at all and maybe just wanted the time to get things in order for the audit. It was also a good job it was the only inspection that day or that would have meant more trauma. I duly walked back to my hotel, cooled off and then walked back and completed the inspection. An early night followed as I was getting picked up at 3am, heading to Paraguay in the morning for the last stop on my South America trip. I was leaving Uruguay with fond memories and is definitely one place in South America that I would gladly go back to.

Chapter 5

Paraguay

Paraguay

Asuncion

The first thing that struck me in Asuncion, the capital of Paraguay, was the heat and humidity. I have been to the Caribbean, Las Vegas, Egypt etc but nothing hit me as much as that did and it had the sort of humidity that without moving, caused sweating and shortness of breath. I was ecstatic to sit in a taxi with air-conditioning for the 30-minute ride to my hotel.

What was apparent was that this was a poor city. The roads had very little tarmac on them, the pavements had cracks and holes in them which made a simple walk hazardous and there was a large homeless gathering about 100 yards from my hotel of about 150 adults and children. They had taken over a road and placed tarpaulin across the buildings for shelter and they all slept on cardboard on the floor. Very unnerving but not threatening, I walked past that area every day and night, but not once did I feel in any danger. The children were all playing quite happily with what little they had, as the adults were going through bins and rubbish for food etc. It was a sobering and surreal experience.

I checked in to my hotel, which considering the surroundings, was actually very good. As I had the afternoon off, I decided to check out the pool, which was situated on the roof top. Again, this was a bizarre experience, as there I was cooking in the incredible heat and then cooling off (at least every five minutes) in the lush pool and at the pool bar, but the view I had was of total poverty and the homeless. I can only imagine what they were thinking whilst looking up at me.

The next morning, my first audit to complete was the hotel I was staying in. This is a bit strange as you go from being a valued guest and feeling wanted, to the nasty hotel inspector who they cannot wait to get rid of. It also might suggest that I would be more lenient if I found something that was not quite right as it was in 'my house', but this was never the case, and everything was generally ok with the inspection.

I had 2 audits to complete on my next to last day in Paraguay. After a short walk, in the shade with a bottle of water, I arrived and completed my first inspection and completed it with remarkably no issues. The second audit was about half a mile away, according to google maps, but not that far from my own hotel so I made the ill-advised decision not to take a taxi but to walk as I would have arrived too early otherwise. Internet signal then disappeared, and I got lost. I asked various people for help but no one spoke English and with no internet I couldn't use the translate app and all I could do was point at the name of the hotel on my paperwork that I was inspecting and they in turn would point up or down the road. This went on for about half an hour, and I was soaked in sweat again. I found a newsagent and bought some more water and went and stood in the shade why I tried to cool, and calm myself, down. I was then shit on by a pigeon with stomach problems and anyone who thinks this is a lucky sign should think again. After buying more water to wash what I could off I was approached by a young man who tried to speak to me. At this point I was expecting the worst, a robbery, a beating or just to laugh at me because he may have owned the ill pigeon, but he spent about 10 minutes with me explaining where the hotel was (in very broken English) and even offered to walk me there which I politely declined. He was superb and to this day I thank him for the help he gave me.

I arrived at the hotel, but I was in a very poor condition. I do not think it was possible to be any wetter with clothes on, I had remnants of the ill pigeon all over me and I was stressed beyond belief. The receptionist gave out a gasp as I walked up, and she called security. After a very bizarre conversation with a Spanish speaking guard, he went and got me a towel to help me dry off and led me back to reception. Now connected to the hotels Wi-Fi, I could communicate with them via the translate app but then the manager arrived and told me to leave as they did not want to be audited! No amount of reasoning with them made any difference, including a call from the UK from the company I was working for, and I eventually left for my hotel after a hugely successful afternoon. It does make you wonder what a hotel has to hide if they refuse to let the hotel inspector in?

Whilst lost earlier I had noticed a Hard Rock Café which was about a 15-minute walk from my hotel. As it was to be my last night in South America, and I had spent the last 3 hours in a cold shower, I thought it would be a nice way to end the trip with some recognisable food and drink as a sort of 'celebration' that I had survived South America. The temperature had now dropped to about 37 degrees, but I was happy, and I was looking forward to my 'celebration'. After walking past the homeless and avoiding all the holes in the pavement I eventually arrived, albeit very sweaty again, at the Hard Rock Café. It was shut. In fact it had never been open as they were still in the process of building it. The first thing they had done is put up a great big Hard Rock Café sign and illuminated it so you could see it from miles away and then maybe sometime in the future they were going to look at the minor detail of fitting it out and opening it. I was now boiling hot, needing food and a cold drink when like an oasis in the desert I spotted a bar. This had the illuminated sign and it was open, so it ticked all the boxes but in fact it was not a bar, it was a casino. As you could imagine in a poor city, this was a rundown seedy casino with some very dodgy looking people inside, but it served good beer and a fairly decent ham toastie. The staff were very pleasant and one of them even sat with me for a while talking about his favourite subjects, Mo Salah and Liverpool football club. That said, I was still glad to get back to my hotel in one piece as after dark it did have a 'watch your back' feel to it.

My last hotel in South America to audit was at 9am, but I was not starting my journey home until 8pm so after checking out of my hotel and getting a taxi, with my suitcase, I arrived at my last appointment in Asuncion. After finding the 1 employee, the housekeeper, who could speak any kind of English and proceeded with the audit, which was all ok but it did include something I had never come across before anywhere in the world, which was a boiler that was fuelled by wood! A 14-storey hotel with about 200 rooms fuelled by wood, that had to be manually re-loaded constantly, in temperatures that a camel would have found excessive! Not forgetting that in the basement of the hotel you have a fire burning 24/7! A simple recommendation of 'get some gas installed asap' was made.

After completing my work at about 11am I wondered how I could fill in the time before I headed to the airport at about 4pm. A gentle walk, I thought, around the city, would let me take in this culture one last time. I could leave my suitcase in the hotel and after all it was only 38 degrees, I was fully dressed, and I was only carrying my heavy man bag/ laptop. I walked about 200 yards, bought a bottle of water, drank it like I had been lost in the desert for 3 weeks and staggered back to the hotel to dry off and sit in the air conditioning. Again, I looked like I had just had a shower with my clothes on. The housekeeper came over and asked if I was ok, to which I replied that as I was British, I was not used to this type of heat or humidity.

'Whereabouts in Britain are you from' he asked, 'Near Liverpool' was my reply, 'ah Mo Salah' was his response.

I asked him what time the buffet restaurant opened, and he advised about 12.30, so after drying off I headed up to the restaurant for some lunch, which was also going to kill some time and keep me out of the heat. No one in the restaurant spoke any English, so after using my translate app the waiter pointed towards a table and then to the food, then to some small weighing scales. After checking my app to see what I had actually asked him for (damn you auto correct) it appeared nothing had been lost in translation. I watched another guest load up her plate, then she walked over to the scales where her food and plate were then weighed, and she paid the waiter accordingly. This, I thought, has got to be the most bizarre procedure in a buffet I had ever seen. After spending 10 minutes picking all the meat out of a stew and only picking the lightest vegetables I could find, with a side plate of salad (the lightest ones) I then headed to the dreaded scales. I also asked for a diet coke (hoping that it was not going to be weighed) and stood in anticipation at the cost. It was less than £4 and that included the drink. I then sat in envy at the other guests eating potatoes.

I arrived at the airport at about 3.30pm. I felt I had to leave the hotel as I was getting more funny looks then normal just sitting there with sweat stains so before they called the hygiene police, I got a taxi for a change of scenery. The check in desk only opened at 5pm but I wanted to try to upgrade to premium/ extra leg room or anything to make the twelve-hour flight to Madrid a bit more pleasurable. So I got in, at that stage, the very small queue and waited the one and a half hours until it opened. Nothing was available, but she did offer a window seat which I took as at least I could possibly get some sleep without being interrupted by anyone.

On boarding the plane I arrived at my seat to find a young woman sitting in it. I re-checked my ticket and mentioned to her that she was in the wrong seat, to which she replied in perfect English, 'I want to sit next to the window'. I then advised her, very politely, that it was my seat and I picked it because I wanted to sit next to the window and that is why I queued up for 1.5 hours. 'Do you mind if I stay here though' she asked. 'Yes, I do mind so please move' was my now more purposely toned response.' 'Pleeaassseee can I stay here?' She said whilst tilting hear head like a puppy dog. 'For fucks sake, get out of my seat' was my reply. She muttered something in I presume Spanish, which I very much doubt was complimentary to me, and moved into the aisle so I could get in. For the next 12 hours until we got to Madrid I sat next to this young woman, never spoke, or even glanced at each other, nor did I get any sleep, mainly in fear she was going to do something unpleasant to me. At least I probably smelt bad so that made me feel better.

After running through Madrid airport, which incidentally is huge, I just managed to check in as the desk was closing, then run the 15 minutes to the gate, via 2 security gates and was virtually the last one on the plane for my connecting flight home to nice cold England. I slept the whole way back to Manchester.

It had been a hell of a 3-week trip.

Chapter 6

Greece

Greece

Greece is a fantastic part of the world and the favourite holiday destination for many Europeans. With its various small islands, quaint buildings and tavernas, mixed with the lovely nature of Greek people and the great weather, I was really looking forward to going back to experience more of it, even though this time I would be working.

Crete

My first destination was to the largest Greek island, Crete, however as it was only just coming into holiday season there were no direct flights from the UK. I have been to Crete before on various holidays and it is a beautiful place so I could not wait to return there, especially as I was going to the opposite side of the island that I have never been to. After getting a very early, 4-hour flight from Manchester to Thessaloniki (mainland Greece), retrieving my luggage and rechecking onto a different airline, I then boarded my connecting flight to Chania Airport, on the west of the island.

The only problem being I was starting to feel unwell. I was hot, headachy and my throat was starting to get sore, but I tried to ignore it, took some pills and had a little snooze until we landed. By the time I had walked through the arrival lounge and collected my hire car I felt awful. My body felt on fire, I could hardly swallow as my throat was so sore and my head was now feeling like a base drum. The plan was to get to my hotel and go straight to bed, with the hope that the next day I would feel good enough to go to work. I put my hotel details in the sat nav and drove for about 20 minutes into the centre of Chania old town, but there soon became another problem. The centre of Chania had now become pedestrianised with all the roads in the centre permanently blocked off, but the authorities obviously forgot to mention this to sat nav developers, so I ended up getting very lost trying to find the closest place to my hotel that I could park. Sat nav also directed me down a one-way street, the wrong way, causing locals to run around flapping their arms in disgust, and I then somehow ended up on the harbour side very close to the water's edge. I was not thinking clearly, I felt ill and at that point I should not have been driving so I decided to park up anywhere I could and call the hotel to see if they could help. They directed me to a car park, about a mile away from the hotel and said it was easier to walk from there. What they did not tell me was the mile walk to the hotel was over loose gravel, which was not invented to pull a suitcase over, whilst feeling ill, in 26-degree heat. By the time I got to the hotel it is no exaggeration to say that I was close to collapsing, I felt that bad. I checked in and was planning on going straight to bed when I noticed, after taking of my top, I was covered from the neck down in a bright red angry rash. I evidently needed to seek medical assistance, so I called reception to see if there was a pharmacy close by which luckily there was, so after changing into cooler clothes, I went to see if they could help. After leading me to a consultation room, the pharmacist asked me take my top off, which I did, and then she shrieked and left the room! Now, my body might be way past Olympic athlete standards, but it does not usually get that reaction. I got dressed again and poked my head out of the door, to see the pharmacist at the opposite side of the shop saying, 'you need hospital' and 'can't come near you as I am pregnant' and was basically ushering me out of the shop like I was carrying the black death or something worse. I returned to my hotel and passed this update on to the receptionist who kindly called the hospital and arranged for me to go there as soon as possible, and as it was only a few hundred yards away I was there in no time. After being examined, poked and prodded by 3 separate doctors I was asked to wait until an ambulance could take me to a dermatology expert who could investigate further. I was sat there thinking, 'Christ, this has escalated quickly' and more importantly 'what is wrong with me'! It was also a very distressing situation to be in, feeling very ill in a foreign hospital, with the language barrier and also being alone. After transferring to another medical practice, and subsequently being examined I was told 'you have 100%, got scarlet fever' and prescribed some horse size pills that I had to take for the next 5 days. No wonder the pregnant pharmacist did not want to be anywhere near me, and no wonder I felt like shit. It was highly infectious, and I was also told to avoid all contact with anyone for a minimum of 48 hours, to not let anyone come into my hotel room i.e. cleaners and to also inform everyone that I had been in contact with over the last 24 hours. I had just been on 2 separate planes with hundreds of people, so the hospital were also going to inform the Greek authorities. I also had to cancel all my audits for the week.

As a start to an exciting planned week goes, this was not right up there with the best.

Quarantined in my tiny hotel bedroom, feeling awful, whilst in the UK they were planning on getting me home as soon as I was allowed to fly, which is 24 hours after the rash has gone, so I had no idea how long I was going to be in this situation. The hotel did not have room service,

77

but if I called down to reception they would go out and get me some water and then leave it outside my door. I then slept, on and off, for about 2 days, feeling genuinely ill and only waking up to take my tablets or go the toilet. On the 3rd day my rash disappeared, and I suddenly felt a lot better. After showering, I ventured out in the evening to the supermarket to get some food and went straight back to the hotel but by now I was feeling back to normal. The UK office now arranged my flight home, but it did mean I had a full day in Chania before I had to leave and from what I have seen, it was a lovely place, especially the harbour area with its bars and restaurants. It was just a shame I never got to see more of it and I also felt very guilty at the total waste of time and money this trip was for all concerned.

After packing up and finding a different route to walk to the car park that had a solid floor, I was already heading back to the airport for my 2 flights home, this time via Frankfurt in Germany instead of Thessaloniki. Whilst I imagine the hotel at this time were boil washing my towels and bedding whilst spraying disinfectant around like they were putting a fire out.

Kalymnos

'Can you go to Kos on Monday, for 2 weeks?' was
the request from the office with the now usual 3
days' notice. 'No problem' came the standard
response from me, as who would not want to go
to there and get paid at the same time, whilst it
was also just about coming into summer season
so the weather would be great as well. Kos is
another small Greek island that I had not been to
before, but I thought if it is anything like the
others, I am sure to love everything about it. As it
turned out this was to be one of my trips that I
would always look back on with fond memories.
I checked my itinerary, and this also included
catching a ferry from Kos to another smaller
island called Kalymnos. Apparently, it was a well-
known destination for rock climbers and 'sponge'
divers, but I had never even heard of it. The plan
was for me to stay there for 3 nights before
returning to Kos for the remainder of the trip.
After catching my early morning flight out of
Manchester to Kos, I caught a cab to Mastichari
bay where the ferry to Kalymnos departed from. I
had a couple of hours to wait until the ferry left
so I found a lovely little restaurant in the bay and
whilst enjoying the stunning views and the
weather, I had a great tuna salad with some
lovely cold wet refreshments. After buying a

ticket and pushing my suitcase up the ferry ramp, I settled down on the nearly empty top deck and enjoyed the fantastic 1-hour crossing of the Aegean Sea to Kalymnos whilst thinking 'holy shit, I am getting paid to do this'! On arrival in the busy port I was met by one of the local tour reps, who was to accompany me during my work on the island, and subsequently took me to my hotel on the other side of the island. I was glad I did not have to drive there as well as the roads got very narrow and undulating the more we drove, and I am also not convinced that any of the locals had actually taken a driving test either the way some of them were driving. The part of the island I was staying in was very remote, but stunning. It reminded me of the film 'Mamma Mia' with its stunning views and quaint little buildings, and even though my hotel was little more than a very small, family run, bed and breakfast, the owner went out of her way to make me feel very welcome. It was just a lovely part of the world to be and why this island is not more well-known amazes me to this day. After venturing out for a meal in the most idyllic setting overlooking the water during the sunset, I returned to my accommodation for an early night ahead of a busy following day.

I was picked up around 9am and my rep took me to my first audit. I always do a little research on the property beforehand just so I know what to expect when I get there i.e. small or large property, swimming pool, water park etc and it also gives me an idea of how long the inspection will take, which was important if you had 3 in a day, which is what I had that day. My research on the first hotel told me it had a pool and also offered half board, so I knew it would have had a kitchen, restaurant etc as well. As we started looking around on arrival, it was quite evident that this small hotel did not have a pool. When I asked the manager 'I thought you had a swimming pool' his reply was 'we do', so I asked him to show me, to which he replied, 'it's not here, it's in my cousins house up the road'. I looked at him in utter amazement, as he proceeded to show me photos of his cousins pool on his mobile phone. Now without getting into the legal ramifications of this i.e. who is to blame if there was an accident in this pool, I was not there to inspect his cousins house. So after deciding with the rep to remove the pool element from the 'what we offer' section of the hotel I continued with the inspection. I did notice that on the outside patio area that the hotel had food menu's on all the tables, so asked the manager if I could see the kitchen. 'We don't have a kitchen' was the reply. 'Well how can you offer food without one' was my obvious reply to which he said, 'I have another cousin, and if a guest orders any food, we ring him up, he cooks it and he brings it here'. Aghast, I asked him who would be to blame if anyone got ill from the food, to which he said, 'it wouldn't happen, my cousin is a good cook'.

It was very quickly obvious that these hotels in Kalymnos had never being audited and up to now I imagine the manager had just completed a form to say what the hotel had to offer, and no one ever visited or questioned it but the current health and safety standards were way below expectations and required a lot of work to put them right.

We moved onto the 2nd audit and when we arrived the manager told us that he knew what hotel we had just been to as someone had called him. This confused the rep and I slightly as we had not mentioned to anyone where we were going after the first hotel, so unless we were being followed, the jungle drums in Kalymnos were definitely alive and well. This hotel did have a pool as advertised, but did not have any lifeguard or signage up to indicate adjacent lifesaving equipment, so I called the rep over and told her that the hotel could always put a big sign up with the wording along the lines of 'If drowning, please call my friend's cousin and he will get here as soon as possible'.

After completing the last audit of the day which had the most bizarre fire exit directional signage ever (if there had of been a fire you would have

82

run around in a circles, then gone up stairs), I was dropped off at my hotel where I decided to get changed and go for a long walk in the sun along the coastline. It was lovely and as the sun was starting to go down, I found a small restaurant that gave me the best view of it all, sat down and waited to be served. The waiter came over and said, 'Hello, I take it you're the auditor from England'! It made us both laugh, and it did confirm that everybody knew everybody here and indeed the jungle drums on Kalymnos were very sophisticated.

I had a great few days on this lovely little island, with genuine lovely people, before I was packing up and heading back to the ferry to Kos, for the remainder of the trip.

Kos

I arrived back in Kos on Thursday lunch time after saying goodbye to the rep in Kalymnos and crossing the Aegean Sea once more. I got a taxi to my hotel, where I was staying in until Monday morning, which was also going to be the only audit I had left before having the weekend off. It was a superb hotel, a massive 5* complex with its own beach and about 5 pools and I thought I had just won the lottery when I arrived at the suite they had given me, with a huge bathroom, separate living room, massive bedroom and a large balcony overlooking one of the pools. My phone rang in my room and it was the manager asking me for a favour, 'could you carry out the audit straightaway as I am busy tomorrow' which was perfect for me as then I had 3 days off in this resort! The audit went like a dream with no issues and I then went straight into holiday mode, got changed and headed for the bar. Friday was spent mainly around the pool and the beach, the weather was fantastic and as the hotel was quite quiet it was easy to get meals, drinks, sunbeds without any hassle. I planned to do the same Saturday, until I opened the curtains that morning and it was hammering down. So what else do you do in a holiday hotel when it is raining? Find the nearest bar of course! I made full use of the 'facilities' that day and it was only when I woke up in the morning feeling like my head weighed 3.5 tonnes, as well as when I went to check out of the hotel on Monday morning and I saw the bill, I realised I had enjoyed them far too much. Sunday reverted to lovely hot sunny weather, so I managed to stay away from the bars until later that afternoon, when I started to feel sort of normal again, but only after collapsing on a sun lounger for most of the day. After enjoying a nice meal in the company of the hotel manager, I settled down for an early night as it was back to work the next day and my hire car was also getting dropped off at the hotel around 8am. Just as I started to drop off to sleep, a loud insect buzzing noise come from inside my ear. I jumped up and turned the light on but could not see the culprit, so turned everything off again and was just dropping off again when it come back inside my ear, buzzing away, so I proceeded to whack myself in the head, in the faint hope of 'getting it'. What followed must have looked like a scene from a Monty Python film. I am shouting 'come here you little bastard' whilst moving round the room, naked, like I was on an army manoeuvre, with my pillow ready to swat it into the next life. This continued for about half an hour. I imagine the little bastard was hiding somewhere watching me, whilst absolutely pissing itself laughing. I never did find it and luckily it did not chew me to bits all night, but it did take me ages to get to sleep as I was in angry stealth mode ready to jump into action for the battle ahead. The little bastard.

The island of Kos is lovely, and it was fantastic drive to the opposite side of the island towards the capital, which bizarrely is also called Kos. I presume when the locals were deciding the capitals name, they had a big argument and couldn't decide on the new name, so the boss man stomped his feet and said 'right, that's enough, if you can't be adult about this and unanimously decide, we will just call it Kos', allegedly. I imagine there is a proper explanation, but this all made sense to me as it played out in my head. I arrived and completed an audit at one of the larger hotels near to the centre of Kos without any problems, and subsequently found my own hotel and checked in. My accommodation was on the outskirts of the capital and was situated directly opposite the beach in a perfect location within walking distance of bars and restaurants.

This is sometimes an odd feeling and does make this job a little strange, but fantastic at the same time. I was staying in a tremendous holiday destination, amongst holiday makers, in perfect settings with perfect weather but I was alone and there to work. It was sometimes hard to distinguish between working and being on holiday, more so than ever whilst I was there in Greece. Do I just get my work done and then go into holiday mode? What if my wife, or my employer for that matter, thought I was having too much of a great time and acting like I was on holiday when I should have been working? Do I have a great time but not tell them I am enjoying it that much? If I finish early is it ok to have a few beers and sunbathe around the pool? Or do I just get a grip and embrace this fortunate position I have been put in? On some trips the word 'holiday' would never even enter my head due to many influencing factors but in Kos it was the first time I had felt this weird sense of belonging. It was obviously never a problem, but I have mentioned it because it was a strange feeling that is evidently hard to explain.

Now without sounding like I want a job working for the Kos tourist board, I cannot say enough good things about the lovely island. The people I come across were fantastic and down to earth, the hotel standards were excellent and for the remainder of my trip I thoroughly enjoyed working during the day and relaxing in the evening. On one of the days I managed to finish the last audit of the day quite early so headed out for a walk along the sea front, stopping every now and then for a drink in the sunshine and then carrying on to the next watering hole. It was early evening by this stage, so I found a restaurant overlooking the beach and settled down looking at the menu. The Greek waiter came over and asked me what I would like, so I just ordered a beer while I was looking through the menu choices. 'Are you from Liverpool?' he asked. 'yes' I replied. Now I was waiting for the normal 'Mo Salah' response when he said, 'are you a Liverpool fan?'. I responded that I was and suddenly before I knew what was going on, he come over to me and started hugging me! He then told me to move tables and indicated I should be sat in front of the TV. Liverpool FC were playing that evening, at home to Barcelona in a Champions League game in a tie that in all likelihood was going to be a dead rubber as Liverpool were already 3-0 down from the first leg, but you never say never. My new best Greek friend then appeared with 4 Liverpool football shirts and proceeded to drape them all over the table that housed the TV and said I was going to get the best seat in the house to watch the match. At this point and for the remainder of the evening, I was the only paying customer in the entire restaurant. I had a lovely meal whilst having my bestie talking to me constantly about his favourite football club and going back and to from the bar for my refreshments, until he reached fever pitch as the game commenced. The game was incredible and by half time Liverpool were winning 1-0 and at this point we were joined by 3 or 4 of the waiters friends who were also fanatical about the football club. As the game continued Liverpool scored again and the volume of the entire restaurant (6 of us) got louder, then Liverpool scored again, and we all started to scream more encouragement at the TV. With about 10 minutes to go Liverpool scored what turned out to be the winner and we all went completely bananas. At the final whistle we were all hugging and singing, then the waiter went to the bar and brought a huge bottle of whisky out and we all thought it was a good idea to all have whisky shots until the bottle was empty. I was totally trashed. I am not sure what time I left, remember if I did the very long walk back to my hotel or got a taxi, but what I do remember is the fantastic night I had spent in Kos with my new Greek friends. Luckily for me the next morning was free, as my first audit got cancelled a few day ago, because it was at least midday before I could remotely operate as a human being again. After completing 2 audits in the afternoon, which luckily included the hotel I was staying in, I had a bite to eat and as I was still in the 'I am never drinking alcohol again' stage, I had a cup of tea and an early night.

The following day I had 3 audits in the centre of Kos, which locally was called the 'old town'. This turned out to be a real tourist hotspot with its markets, bars and restaurants all leading to the lovely Mandraki harbour area with its fishing boats and their 'catch of the day' stalls with lots of freshly caught fish. It was an absolute pleasure to spend the day there, I audited a hotel then went and sat in the sun to have some lunch, then audited another hotel and found a café in the harbour for a cool drink and then completed the last audit before returning to the harbour for my early evening meal whilst watching the sun setting over the Kos coastline. It is possible that late at night this area would get very lively as I did see a fair few nightclubs, but during the daytime it was a beautiful place to be and a fitting way to spend my last full day in Kos.

After returning to my hotel and packing up what I could, I headed back to the restaurant from a few days prior to say goodbye to my football crazy Greeks and to have a few beers. As a perfect working day abroad goes, this was right up there with the best of them.

My last day in Kos involved a lot of hanging around. I checked out of my hotel and drove towards the airport on the opposite side of the island to complete my last audit, which I completed around lunchtime, but I was not flying home until 7pm so I spent most of the afternoon sitting in various bars drinking soft drinks and tea, just killing time. I arrived at the airport around 4.30 and dropped my hire car off and proceeded to check in, only to be told that my flight had been delayed by 4 hours. I then had 6 hours to wait until I could fly home and therefore spent more time drinking soft drinks and tea. It was an unfitting way to end this trip as it had been thoroughly enjoyable from start to finish, but they were definitely the longest 6 hours of my life until I boarded that flight home.

Zante

Late on Friday afternoon I received a call whilst at home, 'can you go to Zante, on Sunday for a week?'. I was by now used to the late notice but even by their standards this was last minute. I agreed, as I always did, and quickly planned for an impromptu week away to a Greek island that I had yet to visit. I arrived at the airport for my very early Sunday morning flight and got into the check-in queue when I heard a loud group of about 15 lads enter the area. I could obviously see one of the guys was dressed in a wedding dress, including veil, and they were all evidently going on to a stag do to somewhere. Behind this group appeared another group of about 10 lads, whilst their 'groom to be' was dressed up as a baby, including a huge nappy and a dummy. I was thinking 'I really hope they are not on my flight'. In the departure lounge I could hear the 2 respective groups drinking themselves silly in the bar whilst singing loudly, and it was still only 6am, and again I prayed that they were not heading to Zante. Obviously, they both were and what followed was a very loud and irritating flight with a load of lads whose main intention was to get very drunk and to be as loud and outrageous as possible. Now I do not want to be a kill-joy but on the same flight there were families with young children and also elderly passengers who had all saved their money and had been looking forward to that holiday and this is what we all had to put up with for nearly 4 hours. Unacceptable in any language, unless your dressed as a baby or a bride and you are with your equally inconsiderate stupid drunk mates it seems. Luckily, no one reacted to this behaviour as it had the potential to go very bad very quickly considering the alcohol, ego's and the pack mentality of these idiots. The flight staff deserve medals for having to put up with this as well, whilst they are also trying to work and keep everyone safe.

I was glad to get of that plane and was looking forward to the peace and tranquillity of my hire car for the drive to my hotel. As I had no audits to carry out on the Sunday, I checked into my hotel and went for a 30 minute or so walk into the centre of Laganas (known as the strip) as the weather was fantastic and I needed to stretch my legs. This was evidently a party destination, with nightclubs and bars reminiscent of Ibiza or Magaluf in their heyday and the pavement outside the bars were littered with 'happy hour' or 'buy one get one free' adverts. One of the signs was proudly advertising a 'Haribo Head

Fucker' for 5 Euros, which must have been fun trying to explain that to your kids, who were probably pointing to the sign saying that they wanted one. As first impressions of a new destination go, I was hugely disappointed, even though I did find a lovely restaurant away from the strip and enjoyed a fair few beers with my evening meal. It is also fair to say that once I had explored and worked around the island over the coming week, my impression changed to a far more positive one.

You could drive from one side of Zante to the other in about an hour and a half, even though my sat nav must have been allergic to main roads as I spent much of that time on single dirt tracks in the middle of nowhere. When I did manage to find a main road though I was joined by lots of holidaymakers on quad bikes who seemed to have little regard for their, or anyone else's safety, but it did look like they were a lot of fun to ride! It was very easy to get anywhere though, and I visited some stunning places around the island like Agios Nikolaos, Alikanas and Planos to name but a few and they seemed a far more tranquil place to enjoy your holiday. Unless you wanted craziness and a 'Haribo Head Fucker', then Laganas was definitely the place for you. The majority of the hotels I audited were relatively straight forward and compliant, until I got to the very last one on the last day. This was a large complex and it transpired there was no fire detection anywhere in the hotel, not even household type battery detectors. You can imagine being on the 6th floor at 3am when some drunk guys, maybe with one dressed as a baby or a bride, 'accidently' set fire to their ground floor room whilst cooking a late-night snack? By the time you are woken up by the commotion, smoke and flames, the chances of you getting out safely are severely limited. We managed to put things in place immediately that reduced this risk and the hotel were then arranging for a permanent fire alarm to be fitted asap. It also highlighted why this job was so important as potentially, lives depended on it.

My last night in Zante was bizarrely spent with a lot of my in-laws who arrived in Zante that day for a birthday celebration. We could not go on their celebration holiday as my wife and I were flying out to America 2 days later for our own holiday, but luckily and totally unplanned, I managed to spend some time with them and the complimentary beer, for one evening at least.

My flight home was problem free and it was soon time to unpack, wash my clothes then re-pack for the Nevada desert and the bright lights of Las Vegas.

Chapter 7

Spain

Spain

Majorca

Just off the east coast of mainland Spain is the
lovely little island of Majorca, the largest island in
the Balearic Islands and a place where I have
been quite a few times on holiday, and once
even for a wedding. I had no hesitation agreeing
to carry out a short trip there, even though it was
before the summer season had started. The only
issue with going out of season to any 'beach
type' holiday destination is there are virtually no
direct flights and your connecting flights are very
rarely with the same airline, so a normal two and
a half hour direct flight from the UK suddenly
becomes a seven or eight hour journey as every
time you landed you had to collect your luggage
and recheck it in all over again with the new
airline, then wait to re-board your new flight.
This particular trip took me from Manchester to
Barcelona, catching a bus to another terminal,
then Barcelona to Palma airport in Majorca.
Now the benefit of going in the offseason is that
the weather was still great, and the resorts were
quiet. This made driving around the island an
absolute pleasure, you still had all the great

views but there was hardly any other traffic on the roads. Most of the hotels were still closed though and therefore at points I thought the whole audit process was pretty pointless at that time of the year. How can you check food hygiene when all the kitchen are shut? How can you check the swimming pool chemical levels are correct when the pool is empty? Some of the hotels took advantage of the quiet season and used this as an opportunity to carry out some refurbishments, so some of them resembled a building site when you turned up to inspect them. It was a simple 'could not audit the pool, hotel closed' type of report which was no benefit to anybody, but I was there to just report back to the UK company on the current standards and as far as I was concerned that is what I did.

My hotel for the week was situated on the outskirts of Palma in a large modern hotel, within walking distance of the beach. It was also to be the location of a work conference for my UK company the following week that I was also due to attend but I ended up in Crete instead, with a last-minute change of plan of course. My accommodation was not on the list to be audited during this trip, but it had some major issues though. The balcony height was insufficient, the corridors were too long without fire doors meaning the distance from your bedroom to the fire escape or a place of safety was too far, but by far the most serious was that the hotel had no fire alarm! It was eight storeys high with no form of fire detection, sounders or break glass. A fire on the 1st floor could have been catastrophic for any of the guests in the hotel. The regulations at that point indicated Spanish hotels were only required to have a fire alarm fitted when they had a refurbishment, which considering it was probably going to burn down fairly soon anyway, wouldn't be too long away. I did wonder though, why as a hotelier would you put your paying guests at such a risk? I discussed this with the UK company, but they subsequently still went ahead with the conference, albeit in a new wing of the hotel that did have fire detection. It didn't sit right with me though as I had to highlight some real minor issues during my audits, e.g. only testing the fire alarm every two months, instead of every month, but my hotel wing didn't even have one to test and I had to sleep there!

A former colleague of mine once said to me 'all hotel managers are lying bastards', which is obviously not correct but as I found in Majorca, some definitely are. I was inspecting a hotel in Cala d'or, on the east of the island, and like with any audit I would always check what the previous report (from probably 1-3 years ago) had highlighted as a failing to see if they had put it right. This particular hotel had been marked down because the bedroom doors were not fire resistant, or 'self-close' by means of a door closure mechanism. If a fire started in a bedroom, the hotel fire alarm would activate (if they had one!) then the occupant could leave the room and the door would automatically close behind them and no fire could burn through the door for at least 30 minutes nor could smoke spread to other parts of the hotel, giving everyone plenty of time to leave the hotel safely and the fire services to arrive and sort out the situation. I asked the manager if they had changed these doors and had the closure device fitted to all the bedrooms, 'yes, of course' he said, 'we had them all done last year at a very big cost'. He then proceeded to show me receipts for the work carried out, but these were obviously all in Spanish so I couldn't understand them, but I took a photo anyway as proof. During our walk round I told him that I needed to see the bedrooms and suddenly he appeared hesitant saying that as they were closed there was nothing to see, so I told him I had to check for other things in the rooms (very true) so I had to see them. On arriving at the first bedroom it was evident that the doors were not fire doors, and no door closure had been fitted. I said to him, 'you told me these had been changed' to which he replied 'yes', so I responded with 'but they have not been changed have they?', 'no' he replied! Slightly bemused I continued, 'so why did you tell me they had been changed?' to which he replied, 'I was hoping you were not going to check'. 'Not going to check! It's my fucking job to check you lying incompetent bastard' is what I really wanted to say, but obviously didn't as this would be frowned upon by someone in the UK office. I calmly explained the importance of why I was checking these items, the potential lives it could save, and he fully agreed with me, like he probably did with the last 4 auditors who had visited. It bloody annoyed me that in effect, he wanted me to sign off the hotel as 'compliant' when it was anything but and if the worst did happen, I would have some very high level conversations with some very important people which potentially could end up with me in a cell. It was that serious. I never translated them, but I imagine that the 'receipts' for the works were probably a delivery note for baked beans. I finished the audit by checking absolutely everything in minute detail, left the hotel, and sent my report in the knowledge that he was probably not going to change a thing. The lying bastard.

After arriving back at my hotel I went for a stroll to find a restaurant, but the whole resort was still closed, with only a small newsagent that was open for business. I bought myself a mini picnic and went back to my room to sit on my balcony enjoying the views whilst I 'enjoyed' my evening meal of crisps and chocolate. After a quiet night in the hotel bar it was off to sleep, conscious of the lack of fire alarm the whole time whilst wondering if I could abseil from the 8th floor with some knotted sheets.

It was no surprise I woke up early, so I got myself up and out and started my drive to the opposite side of the island to Port de Pollenca. After a beautiful scenic drive I arrived at my only audit of the day, which as the season did not start for another week it was still closed, and I had already noted that this hotel had been marked down on the last inspection for lack of fire doors in the corridors (if they are too long they need to be separated by fire doors to limit the spread of smoke) so entered the property to meet the manager. The Manager did not speak one word of English so we were joined by another member of staff who could translate, and we proceeded with the audit. I asked about the fire doors and if new ones had been fitted to which the reply, via the translator, was 'they are being fitted right now, and they will all be installed before we re-open next week'. No problem I thought, I can catch up with progress during my accommodation walk-round. After inspecting the empty pool, the empty restaurant and the empty kitchen areas I was steered towards the accommodation block on the ground floor and true to their word there was 2 men with 2 large fire doors in the corridor, but surprisingly they were not doing anything with them and I got a weird feeling that they were just stood there waiting for me. I said 'hello' to them both and they both returned pleasantries, but they continued to just stand there. I told them that they could carry on, in a 'don't let me stop you' kind of way and they seemed to be looking at the manager for guidance, who was by now was ushering me along the corridor. It was an odd atmosphere, but I carried on with the audit and eventually ended up on the 1st floor. At this point I was met with 2 more men and 2 more doors, who were also not working and just seemed to be stood there waiting for me. Again, I said 'hello' and they returned the welcome but again they just stood there. I asked the manager, via the translator, why they were not working, and the reply was 'the noise might disrupt me during my inspection. I can smell bull-shit a mile away and at this point I also noticed the 2 men had no tools whatsoever to even fit the door and suddenly the penny dropped and I quickly made an excuse that I had left something in a ground floor bedroom and despite the delaying tactics of the manager, quickly went to the ground floor again. Of course the 2 guys and the 2 doors on the ground floor were nowhere to be seen. The hotel staff had gone to the effort of moving the same set of new fire doors around the building to make it look like they were fitting them, to keep me happy and subsequently report that everything was ok. They had bought, or possibly removed, 1 set of fire doors to dupe me into ticking the 'all ok' box. 'Do you think I am that stupid?' I asked the manager directly to which he replied, in good English as well, 'they are due to be fitted over the next week'. So he also spoke English, the lying bastard. When I challenged him again, he admitted that he wanted me to think the doors were being fitted but promised me they would be fitted before they opened and of course I believed him. Why not just say that to me from the offset? Unless I see everything in place I would not dream of 'believing' any hotel 'will' do anything. The whole audit is very black and white with no middle ground. They either have, and you can see it, or they have, and they can prove it with documentation.

I did begin to wonder that by the 6th floor they would have either ran out of local volunteers to stand with the doors, of it would be the same men in disguises, with wigs and fake moustaches etc and even now I wish I had not said anything to see how chaotic it would have got. The lying bastard.

The hotel managers who lie during the audit are not understanding that the work we do is for the protection of everybody, the guests, the tour operators, and the hoteliers alike. If there was an incident and all recommendations had been adhered to, it would greatly reduce the risk of personal injury, or even death, to guests. But from a hoteliers perspective, if the advice is ignored, they are probably breaking some local laws so would face those consequences, the damage to the building, the amount of time they could not trade, Local and national PR, injury claims etc. If they put the same effort into putting things right as they did to arrange 'moveable doors' on an audit, then everybody and every business would be a lot safer. Rant over.

After finding a lovely restaurant on the way back to Palma I decided to spend the evening wandering around Palma sea front, which just out of season was a wonderful place to be. Without the chaos of mid-summer, the extreme heat, and gangs of holiday makers it was a tranquil setting that I wished I could have bottled up to take everywhere with me.

After another night in the hotel, where knotted bed sheets were again not required, I made my way to an audit that turned out to be a total waste of time. It was a huge property on the outskirts of Palma that was under major refurbishment and the whole area was a total building site. They had decided to relocate all of the 3 swimming pools, relocate all of the 4 kitchens, build an extension, and refurbish all existing bedrooms, so suffice to say 'could not audit, under refurbishment' was the answer to virtually every question. Pointless, and my trousers were also filthy. That said, once it had been completed, it would have been a stunning property to stay in for your holiday.

My short stay in Majorca was coming to an end and as expected I had enjoyed my time there, albeit with some very frustrating moments. Whilst I was expecting to return to Palma the following week for a work conference, I received a call before I left for home to ask me to go to Crete instead, some 48 hours later. So I got my flight from Palma to Edinburgh, then after a 4 hour wait, a short flight home to unpack, wash, dry, iron and repack my clothes for my next trip.

Costa Del Sol

After receiving my customary 3 days' notice, I was heading to the Costa Del Sol on the south coast of Spain for 3 weeks. A favourite destination for many holiday makers around Europe, but it has a distinct 'British' feel to it as most bars and restaurants cater for the British palate and as most of the low cost airlines fly there it is also within easy reach of the UK with only a 2-3 hour flight time. Unless you go just out of season like I did, so it was a flight from Liverpool to Belfast, a 3 hour wait, then Belfast to Malaga. It was a bit surreal whilst waiting in Liverpool's John Lennon airport though. It was 9am and very quiet with hardly anybody around when all of a sudden there was a loud commotion through the departure lounge and then Steven Gerrard (ex-Liverpool football club captain) appeared as he was being walked through with a police escort to I presume a private jet to take him back up to Glasgow where he was managing Glasgow Rangers football club. Once it had calmed down a bit, I found a seat and was subsequently joined in the area by 2 other guys who sort of looked familiar. It turned out they were Kaka and Andrea Pirlo, 2 Italian football legends! It transpired (using google!) that the day before there was some sort of charity football match between Liverpool legends and an AC Milan legends side and all these guys were making their way home. There was a fair bit of 'spot the football legend' going on and it did help to pass the time before I boarded my flight with lots of Liverpool fans who were returning home to Belfast after watching the game.

This trip was to be a little different to the normal 1-2 full audits a day and initially I was also to be joined by a new starter who was going to shadow me. This trip was all about checking that the deficiencies from the last audits that had been completed or were still outstanding. So this meant, for example, I would go into a hotel just to check that they had completed a fire test in the last month, or the cracked tile around the pool had been replaced, but not check for anything else. In reality it was going to be a lot of driving and a lot of waiting around between appointments unless they would let me see the few issues straight away, but I was not to concerned as I was getting paid and the weather was going to be lovely.

After a problem free airport transfer in Belfast, I arrived into Malaga airport around 7pm but my new starter colleague was not arriving from London until 10pm so I was no hurry to do anything quickly once I had landed. It was probably the opposite of what everyone else normally does on arriving abroad. As everyone else were crowding around the luggage carousel waiting for their luggage, I was sat waiting until they had all moved away. The big queue at the car rental kiosk didn't bother me as I found a coffee shop and chilled out there until there was no queue. I ambled up to the empty car rental kiosk and was signing all the normal paperwork when the operative told me of a very special offer on sat nav rentals, 'only 10 euro for three weeks hire' and I instantly, stupidly, agreed to this fantastic deal as I looked directly at the gift horse in his mouth. He gave me directions to the car park area my hire car was located and off I went with time on my side, out of the terminal and a good 15-minute walk away. The car was fine, but I noticed it come with a factory fitted built in sat nav which worked perfectly. At this point I should have put the rented sat nav in the boot and forgot about it, but no, as I had the time, I thought I would take it back and tell them that I obviously didn't need it. So after another 15-minute walk back to the terminal, I realised the car rental kiosk was 'air side' and you could not just walk back in, so after finding a security operative who advised me where I had to go to regain entry, I found myself in another queue to be scanned and checked before I was allowed back in. At this point it transpired my flight ticket would allow me back into the departure lounge for a period of 24 hours from landing. My flight ticket though, was in my bag, which was in the car, 15 minutes away. So after a further 2 x 15 minutes' walk, I got back into the now larger queue with my used flight ticket to gain re-entry.

There was now a huge queue at the car rental kiosk as a lot of flights had just landed and therefore a queue that wasn't going to go down quickly as all the luggage carousels were also very busy. After about an hour I got to the front of the queue and the operative refunded my 10 euros, whilst ignoring my question about the 'special offer' when I already had one in the car that they were providing. It was now 10.30pm and luckily my colleagues flight had been delayed by 45 minutes, so I just had enough time to get back to the terminal arrival point to greet her as she walked out. 'sorry about your wait, were you bored for 3 hours?'. Through gritted teeth I responded 'no, I was fine thanks, I kept myself busy'.

After walking back to the car, and eventually finding the hotel and checking into our relevant rooms, it had just passed midnight. It was a budget hotel relatively close to the airport that we were only staying in for 1 night, but unfortunately it didn't have any air conditioning in the room, and it was like an oven. It was still warm outside, but even hotter inside the room so I opened the windows as far as they would go and settled down for a very uncomfortable night's sleep.

I woke up and felt something crawling on my neck so instinctively smacked it with the palm of my hand and proceeded to put the bedside light on. I don't know how big that thing on my neck was, but when squashed it made a hell of a mess of the white bed sheets, my hand, and my neck. I went into the bathroom and it looked like I had been attacked by a pack of wolves with blood all over me and various lumps beginning to appear on my arms, neck, and legs. I put the main bedroom light on, and the walls were covered by the entire cast of the Bugs Life film who had evidently been 'feeding' all night. Little bastards.

Working as an auditor abroad you become comfortable in your own company and apart from the pre-arranged appointments, I enjoyed the freedom to basically plan my days. I could eat and drink what I wanted, when I wanted, stay in or go out, be lively or be quiet, etc. so when for the first time I was shadowed by someone else it was a strange feeling that I had to consider someone else! Some days I would only eat biscuits until my evening meal, on others I would have a full restaurant meal for lunch and only alcohol for evening meal! Should I behave any different now I am being shadowed? What if my colleague goes back to the office and the boss asks them how they had got on, 'oh it was great, we got smashed every day and only ate biscuits' would have no doubt end with a word in my ear but then again 'we had 3 square meals a day and he was professional throughout' would have them double check it was actually me that she was shadowing. I decided to go with the 'this is me, like it or lump it' approach and to be fair we got on great and had some good laughs at each other's expense, especially the time we were chatting away and did not notice the upcoming speed bump and hit it at probably double the speed I should have. My colleague flew back to the UK only a few days later though and I am not really sure what she learnt from me, apart from I swore a lot, drank too much, and moaned the lumps on my body were very itchy.

The first few days were spent around Malaga city which was very busy and chaotic like most cities before moving on to the far quieter and picturesque Benalmadena. I was probably visiting 5-6 hotels a day around the area that were completed in no time as I was only in each hotel for about 10 minutes each checking the odd random thing, so most afternoons it felt like I was on holiday, just sitting around the harbour whilst people watching and drinking. My hotel was on a small peninsula on the beach, so the views were incredible all around the hotel, but to sit on my balcony with the waves crashing into the rocks below with a cold beer at sunset was bliss and the only thing missing to make it perfect was my wife. I called her and spontaneously booked for her to come out in the middle of my trip and stay with me for a few days, as she could work remotely using the hotel's Wi-Fi whilst I was out, then spend the weekend and evenings together 'getting smashed and eating biscuits'.

For the next few days and over the weekend I was based in Marbella, a supposed destination for the rich and famous and the people who pretended or wanted to be. The marina area is stunning though, with its luxury yachts and ridiculously overpriced bars and restaurants it was definitely upmarket and worth a visit if you are in the area, even if it is just to watch people pretending that they are rich and important whilst sounding like they are auditioning for the next series of 'The only way is Essex'. Some of the hotels I visited in the area were stunning and luxurious with a price to match, but there was equally nice places within a few miles away that did not carry the same price tag as Marbella. Sometimes you don't get what you pay for, but each to their own and in certain circles 'going to Fuengirola' does not have the same ring to it as 'going to Marbella'. As you can probably gather, it wasn't my cup of tea, but I am still glad I had the chance to visit.

Next up was a drive from Marbella to the area around Estepona, around 15 miles from

Gibraltar. It was a golfers paradise with lots of sunshine and quality golf courses in the area, including Valderrama which hosted the Ryder cup golf tournament, whilst the views towards Gibraltar were fantastic on a clear sunny morning. I checked out some issues at a few of the golf hotels then I had my lunch overlooking the golfers as they teed off on a course that I have only seen before on TV. Right then it did feel like 'this is the best job in the world', but as expected something always fucks it up and all of a sudden it started spitting with rain, then came really heavy rain, then thundering, then lighting and that was that beautiful moment gone and before long I was back on the motorway, with my windscreen wipers in full flow, for the 1 hour drive to Torremolinos.

By the time I had arrived in Torremolinos it was clear blue sky and hot again, which meant some of the bites that I was gifted with on my first night were really starting to irritate, especially the one on my wrist. I was using the normal bite cream, but it wasn't doing anything to help so decided to keep an eye out for a chemist to see if they could prescribe anything stronger, but in the closed season this was easier said than done. I eventually found my hotel, but it did not have any car park. I stopped outside the hotel to ask where I could park and they gave me a map to firstly drive around the one-way system, then park, then walk for 20 minutes or so back to the hotel. I am not sure if the bites on my body, or that my tranquillity was shattered by the weather during my lunch, was causing me to be particularly cranky but I refused to stay there. I called the UK company to rant about them booking me a hotel that had no parking and to be fair they agreed and told me to find my own accommodation and they would pay for it. Perfect. I found a really nice hotel on the sea front about 20 minutes' walk from Fuengirola, which was also more central to my visits for the next week or so, and as my wife was joining me in a few days I also wanted it to be nice for her as well. I went back to Torremolinos the next day to work and personally I am glad I wasn't staying there even though it is a hugely popular holiday destination, as in my view it was just too British. If I go anywhere on holiday, I want to experience that particular countries culture, food etc but this felt like I was in Blackpool or Brighton as nearly everyone I come across outside the hotels were British, the pubs had all British food and drink and apart from the weather, it didn't feel very Spanish at all. Now I understand that many people like these sort of 'home comforts' whilst on holiday and even I get excited if I see Guinness sold anywhere abroad but I also want to 'feel' like I am on holiday whilst embracing different cultures, not sitting in the sun drinking British beer and eating British food, with British people whilst I am on holiday. I fully understand though that I am probably in the minority and the popularity of the area pays testament to that. Each to their own and all that.

The next day I was in up in hills visiting the beautiful little village of Mijas, about a 20-minute drive from Fuengirola. The first thing I noticed is how much cooler it was there compared to Fuengirola, which is to be expected as it is situated nearly 500m above sea level, but the views over the coastline from such a high vantage point were awesome and more than made up for the drop in temperature. After a quick hotel visit, I then spotted a chemist which considering my arm was now turning into the size of my leg, was a welcome sight. When it was my turn at the counter I showed the pharmacist and he let out a bit of a gasp and called one of his colleagues over who also made some 'wow' sort of sound and then asked me if he could take a photograph of it! Now I am not sure if my arm is now on some sort of bizarre insect bite porn site as I happily agreed, and he clicked away whilst his colleague went to get the industrial strength bite cream from the presumably locked cage in the guarded basement. It worked a treat though and within a few days it had gone from looking like 'this will kill you' to the 'that looks sore' stage which was a marked improvement. After some lunch and another quick hotel visit it was back to Fuengirola for my weekend off and after a quiet evening meal it was off for an early night as I was picking my wife up from the airport early morning.

I was in Costa Del Sol for nearly 3 weeks and it only rained twice, the time in Estepona at the golf course and the day I picked my wife up from the airport. I had been telling her how fantastic the weather was, telling her to bring sun cream, bikinis etc but when I met her, she had the look of 'you lying bastard' on her face whilst the rain was dripping of her head. Luckily though it cleared up in the afternoon and also stayed nice for the rest of her stay, and we had a thoroughly nice weekend catching up.
One thing that got very annoying was whilst siting outside a restaurant enjoying a lovely meal was the so called 'looky looky' men who are trying to flog you sunglasses, hats, t-shirts, DVD's etc. These are usually African men and they just stand at your table trying to sell you stuff, that granted is very cheap but probably very fake, whilst I was trying to have a romantic meal with my wife who I had not seen for nearly 2 weeks. A polite and often repeated 'no thank you' was generally ignored until he had gone through the

list of things he was selling, and as soon as he got the message and left, another seller appeared, and you went through the whole process again, and again, and again. Now I understand they are probably very poor and whatever money they do get is probably sent home to their families, but it is illegal to sell anything in Spain without a vendor license and as most of these African men are probably illegal immigrants anyway, they are not going to have one. I was just as surprised that the restaurants and bars don't get rid of them either as they are clearly harassing their customers to the extent that on a few occasions we chose to eat inside as we were far less likely to be bothered by them, even though some of them did manage to venture inside as well.
It was a great few days though and a nice little break for her as well, she also mastered the 'remote working' around the pool whilst catching some sun! It was great to see her, and also have some company, so when we said our goodbyes it was far less emotional than usual as I was also going to be home within a week.

After a few more days working around Fuengirola and returning to what now seemed a quiet and empty room in the hotel, I headed to Nerja, about 30 miles east of Malaga. My hotel was centrally located with parking, but they forgot to mention the car park was 500 yards away and was not free. There was signs up everywhere stating 5 euros a day, but I could not find anyone to pay this to on arrival. As most of the hotels I was inspecting were walkable from mine, I left the car there for 3 days so was expecting to pay someone 15 euros when I eventually left. Nerja is lovely and a lot quieter than the more central and well-known resorts, with some stunning views from the many vantage points around the town. The first hotel I was inspecting looked familiar and I realised it was a hotel that my wife and I had stayed in during one of our very early holidays together, and then I remembered the initial problems we encountered there! We had booked on-line for a 5-day break and also booked a private taxi for the hour or so journey from the airport as we would not be landing until 11pm, so printed off all of our paperwork and headed off for a nice break. When we landed there was no sign of a taxi, so I called the 24-hour tour operator help line who advised us to get another taxi, keep the receipt and claim the money back, which was no problem. We got to the hotel around midnight who then advised us that we had arrived a day early and the hotel was full. Basically, our paperwork, vouchers, confirmation was all correct as per our booking, but for some reason the hotel had the wrong dates and only had us down for staying for 4 days. After various phone calls between all parties it was confirmed that the tour operator had screwed up and give the hotel the wrong dates, but because the hotel was full they 'made' us a bedroom in the form of the cleaners room, complete with mops and buckets, and put 2 single beds in there. Suffice to say the room was filthy and we both stayed fully dressed whilst we had a few hours' sleep. The next day we moved into our proper bedroom and the rest of the break was great.

The inspection was fine and the manager, who seemed to take my previous story quite personally, treated me to a lovely lunch while unnecessarily apologising repeatably when it wasn't even his fault. The next few days I spent in Nerja were lovely and hassle free, with the evenings spent in a closely located Irish bar and a few great restaurants.

When I left I made my way back to the carpark to find a few guys walking around looking like they were collecting money from people who had just arrived in their cars, so I waved at them and said 'hello' but they ignored me so I got in the car and drove off. Now I doubt I am on 'Costa Del Sol's most wanted' list, but I probably owe someone 15 euros and I doubt if they will ever get it.

I then drove further down the coast to a place called Almunecar for 1 hotel inspection, where not a lot of people spoke any English, but the area was nice with a lovely long beach, before driving 70 or so miles to Torremolinos for my last night before flying home. I was staying in a hotel that I had previously inspected right on the sea front, and on check in the manager recognised me and instantly upgraded my room and put me on all inclusive. Suffice to say the last night was a little messy with free food and beer until my body could not take any more. After a lazy and very quiet morning, I headed back to where it all started, Malaga airport, for my return flight home.

My 3 weeks in Costa Del Sol were complete.

Chapter 8

Morocco

Morocco

Well, what can I say…. The 5-week Morocco trip was to be the longest I have been away from home. Initially the trip had also included going to Tunisia for a few days but that got cancelled at the last minute due to the collapse of Thomas Cook holidays.

So I started my Morocco journey in Liverpool airport, after a very emotional goodbye to my wife, with a flight to Amsterdam on route to Casablanca. I have been on holiday to Amsterdam many times, including a stag party with 20 Irish friends so I am fully aware that everyone is going for a great time to do whatever takes your fancy and to be honest with few limitations. It is an amazing cosmopolitan city and the vibe and people watching are second to none. Most of my fellow passengers were in great spirits and at least half of them were literally, full of spirits. Now this is the thing here, they are going on holiday with their friends, loved ones etc but I was going to work. Once I had landed in Casablanca, I was picking up a hire car so there was absolutely no alcohol for me! I suddenly felt like the sober driver on a night out ferrying friends around (to be fair that very rarely happens!) or a normal Saturday night shift for a taxi driver. It was an 'interesting' and lively 1-hour flight until we landed in Schiphol airport, which incidentally is one of the largest and busiest airports I have been in. After transferring onto a great Air Maroc flight, via some airport fast food, I was heading to Morocco.

Casablanca

Casablanca sounds exotic, like the old Humphrey Bogart and Ingrid Bergman film with the same name, it has a certain enticing appeal and I was very much looking forward to arriving and experiencing its charm. As it turned out it is nothing like that and in fact, they didn't even go to Casablanca to film the movie, it was all done in California.

I landed around 10pm. Much to my dismay there were no signs in English. Now I appreciate I am in North Africa, where the main language is French, followed by Arabic, but I thought in the airport there may be at least some pointers that would help English speakers find their way. A simple 'Rent a car, this way' would have been useful, but unless you understood French or Arabic you had no choice but to ask people, who also didn't understand or speak English. As it was late there were no Sim card outlets open, so internet and translate apps were useless. I did the whole pretending to drive a car motion, with my imaginary steering wheel and gear stick and was eventually pointed in a certain direction by a few different people. I ended up in the Airport long stay car park surrounded by non- hire cars. I walked back to the arrival lounge and found 3 soldiers on patrol, so I went through the whole process of pretending to drive again and was directed to a different part of the airport car parks. I arrived and noticed all the cars had stickers in them stating which hire car company they belong to, perfect so I thought, I was in the right place. Eventually I was approached by a car park attendant and it transpired that I had to go back into the terminal and sign the forms first, then return with the keys to pick up my car. The whole process from landing to getting into my car took about 2 hours, a lot of walking (with suitcase) and it was 30 degrees. I sat in the car with the A/C on full blast to gather my thoughts when it was apparent, without internet, that none of my sat nav apps, google maps etc were going to work. Using my own UK networks internet would have cost the same as purchasing a small yacht, so I went back to the terminal, connected to the free Wi-Fi, and downloaded an offline sat nav app, which seemed to work ok. I set off for the 30 minutes or so journey to the centre of Casablanca to find my hotel. The new app turned out to be useless though as during its development it obviously missed some things out, like minor roads and other stuff they believed unimportant like roundabouts or toll booths. Also the GPS, without internet, was placing me anywhere within a 3-mile radius. Having checked online before I left home to see what currency was accepted in Morocco and apart from the obvious local currency of Dirham, it did say Euros were commonly used, but this turned out to be poor information. I stopped at an unexpected toll booth and asked how much, but the reply was in French, I think, but I did make out the word 'Dirham', the local currency. I explained I only had euros, but the reply was only 'Dirham', so I gave him 10 euros and explained again I had no Dirham. He muttered something, which I doubt was complimentary, got up and left his booth. At this point all the cars behind me were being very patient, by shouting out of their windows and pressing the car horn relentlessly. The toll booth operator eventually returned and gave me some Dirham as change and the barrier went up, but in all the excitement I then stalled the car as a parting gift to my new friends behind me.

I knew my hotel was right in the middle of Casablanca so just followed all the road signs (in French or Arabic) to 'Casablanca' and eventually against all the odds and after a quick chat with a policeman on a checkpoint, I somehow found my hotel. I had only stopped to again ask someone for directions, which in Casablanca at 1am is probably not a good idea, when I saw the hotel down a side street. I left the car where it was, checked in and went straight to bed as I had an audit at 9am the next day.

Using Wi-Fi in my hotel it looked straight forward in finding my 1st audit in Morocco. What I hadn't accounted for is the traffic and the mentality of Casablanca drivers. Traffic light use was optional, everyone's vehicle indicators must have been broken, it is customary to press your vehicle horn repeatably for no apparent reason and everyone, in general, had a total disregard for their own life and others. Pedestrians were no better and crossed any road at will, with or without a pedestrian crossing (that no one took any notice of anyway). Add to this that I was driving on the wrong side of the road to what I am used to, in a car on the opposite side regarding controls, steering wheel etc. Also, at every set of traffic lights, the car was surrounded by African immigrants selling anything from tissues and hair gel to crisps and sunglasses, whilst some were just begging for money whilst holding their baby with an empty bottle in their hand. This was both upsetting and intimidating, even though I was in my locked car. It was not a good mix and how I survived the following 5 weeks of driving in Morocco was a feat in itself.

I arrived at my first inspection to be told I was over a month early and the paperwork I had was incorrect. This is usually a ploy to get rid of me, but after checking with the UK office, they were indeed correct, and I had been sent there a month early by 'an error in the office'. It did buy me some time though to find a phone shop and get a sim card for the 5-week duration and I also exchanged some currency. Onto the next audit with sat nav was a whole lot easier but only in terms of when I went wrong (which was often) it redirected me but the general stress of driving anywhere was unbelievable. At the end of the day when I got back to my hotel it didn't just feel like I had been to work, it felt like I had survived to fight another day.

All the hotels I inspected had 'free parking' on their website, so I thought at least when I get there that part would be easy. In reality though it wasn't that simple. The hotel had cones up outside their hotel so no one else could park there and on arrival you pressed your horn and the doorman would come out and ask why you wanted to park there. If your explanation was satisfactory, he would remove a few cones and you would park as close as possible, we are talking millimetres, to the car in front and hand him your keys. When you are ready to leave, he would move all the other cars out of the way and away you went. There were spaces for about 6 cars, in a 240-bedroom hotel, in a one-way street that was wide enough for 2 cars, 1 parked up and one for the flow of traffic. So when you turned up at the hotel you immediately stopped all traffic flow why you sorted out your parking, which was more complicated as the doorman generally didn't speak English, so I am desperately getting my translate app working so he understood and removed the cones before all the people behind me spontaneously combust in a barrage of horns and shouting. If there were no spaces available for me (oh fuck its 'the hotel inspector'!), they would move someone else's car, to god knows where, so I could park up but this obviously took a little longer just to enhance my growing friendship with more new pals behind me. I completed about 50 audits in my time in Morocco and this procedure was the norm in about half of them.

I initially spent about 3 days in Casablanca auditing and eventually after an early morning inspection I was heading up to Tangier, about a 4-hour drive away. After the utter chaos of city driving, this was bliss as the motorway was virtually empty, the sun was shining, and it was probably the first time I had felt relaxed for days. There were lots of speed cameras dotted along the roadside to keep me from enjoying it too much, but I found long distance driving a god send to 'switch off' for a while. After stopping at a service area, which was basically a shack selling sweets, a toilet, and a praying area, I was approaching the centre of Tangier when my sat nav indicated I would need to park up and walk to my destination- my hotel.

Tangier

Tangier is situated at the top of Morocco, opposite the south of Spain and Gibraltar. My accommodation was a Riad, situated in a Medina. Now at the time this meant very little to me but was to impact me immensely as I toured the country.

A Riad is a small traditional Moroccan guest house situated inside a walled city, the Medina, that for tourist purposes was basically a large market in narrow alleyways. My sat nav was very correct in saying I had to walk the final bit of the journey, but from the car park to my Riad was about a mile walk, through the narrowest of cobblestone alleyways (perfect for pulling a suitcase in 30 degree heat) and as soon as you entered the walled city you lost all internet connection and any sense of direction. The Alleyways are like a walled rabbit warren, with no logic to its layout and even when I did have

Wi-Fi, none of these alleyways showed up on google maps etc. The market sellers were selling everything from knock off designer clothing to live chickens and fish (that were killed and cut up at the stall) and therefore the general smell, in that heat, was unbelievable. Scooters were also zooming everywhere and then you would come face to face with a donkey pulling a narrow trailer full of garbage. It was surreal and the level of noise was already giving me a headache. As a white English man, sweating profusely and pulling a suitcase over cobblestones I have no idea why I must have stood out (!) but the moment I stopped I was approached by a 'local helper' to see if I needed any help and they were relentless. If you asked for directions, they only wanted to take you there, for money of course and would not just tell you how to get there. If you walked away, they would follow. I eventually asked him how much he wanted to take me to my 'hotel' and he said '5 Dirham', which is about £1, so I obviously agreed as I was losing the will to live and it was far cheaper than getting arrested for having a total breakdown. I followed him for about 10 minutes and true to his word I was now at my accommodation, I paid my dues and off he went to find another lost and unhappy soul. Now this was no normal entrance to a hotel, there was no sign, it was just a door with a number on, that luckily matched the address I had so I nervously knocked and waited.

The door opened and the only way to describe inside it is by comparing it to the Tardis from Doctor Who. Inside there was a large courtyard, surrounded by plants and central fountain, with the roof missing and this was definitely not what I was expecting. I was shown to my room which was on the 1st floor (no lift, just narrow stairs) and entered my 'traditional Moroccan Riad' room. It was awful! It was about 3m x 3m, no windows or air conditioning and a very small bathroom area. It was like a prison cell but at least prison cells have a window! The lock on the inside of the door was similar to a rabbit hutch lock and if someone had of leant on the door it would have opened no bother (therefore I had my suitcase up against the door whenever I was inside). You locked the outside of the door with a padlock and it felt like I was staying in a broom cupboard with a toilet. Why, I thought, would anybody 'really' like to experience this traditional accommodation? I appreciate I was working, but if I had gone on holiday to Morocco and paid good money for this, I would be hugely disappointed. As I was there for 5 days I quickly unpacked and then headed out to a late afternoon audit. My Riad owner gave me a map of the medina and tried to give me some directions, openly admitting I would get lost and I would end up asking a 'local helper' for assistance nearer to my destination and that is exactly how it panned out. I found it amazing that these Riads had no signs or directions, but maybe the locals wanted it this way so that the 'local helpers' were always in employment? Every time I was 'helped' we had the same conversation. Where are you from? 'Liverpool' I would reply. 'Mo Salah' was the response 100% of the time. As mentioned earlier, Mo Salah is an Egyptian footballer, but more importantly to them, a Muslim who is revered and well known around the world and is currently playing for Liverpool Football club. I imagine if you're a fan of another football club in Liverpool, this conversation would have got tiresome very quickly!

Working from the scheduled itinerary, I would be spending my first weekend off whilst in Tangier and to be honest it was a far nicer place than my first impressions. The beach area was lovely, with lots of bars and restaurants and during the daytime the medina was a fascinating, bustling, and lively place to be. At night time, especially after a few drinks, you had to have your wits about you as there was an 'undertone' type atmosphere in the alleyways but over the course of my 5 days there my need for a 'local helper' disappeared as I found my bearings. After a couple of more days auditing around Tangier, which included some fabulous Riads that were far superior to mine, I was heading to Rabat, the capital of morocco, for 1 audit.

Rabat

Rabat is Morocco's capital city but only the 7th largest. As the political and administrative capital it is not exactly on anyone's tourist list but in the same breath it also gives you a 'real feel' to Morocco. Nothing there appears to be fed by tourism so what you see is not for your benefit, like many touristy areas, it is how life is really like. It was only a fleeting visit to carry out 1 audit in a hotel where no one spoke a word of English, they obviously didn't want me there and the standards were terrible, but I still left with fond memories of Rabat as I felt I had seen the real Morocco. I was now heading back to the chaos of Casablanca for 2 nights.

Casablanca (take 2)

Luckily, I was returning to the hotel I had previously stayed in (so I only got lost 6 times before I found it). I pulled up outside the hotel, but there was no spaces, or cones, free so I hit

the horn until the doorman come out and told
him I was staying in the hotel and needed to
park, whilst I could hear the relentless blasts of
horns from the cars behind me as I had stopped
the traffic. The doorman eventually reappeared
and moved 'someone's' car and left me enough
space to cram my little Peugeot into.

My 2nd audit the next day was one of the most
bizarre inspection I have ever done. I had
checked the map and both hotels I was
inspecting that day were in walking distance from
mine so there was no need to try and drive
through the streets which instantly lowered my
blood pressure. The first audit was a 5* hotel and
was perfect in every way, an immaculate hotel,
they spoke English, nothing was wrong, they
were genuinely pleased to have me there and
were very accommodating. I arrived at the 2nd
audit stress free and feeling very positive,
probably the first time since arriving in the
country. The first issue was no one spoke English,
but I have an app for that! So after explaining,
through the app, to the receptionist who I was
and my audit appointment etc I was asked,
through the app, to sit and wait. I was given
some mint tea (most hotels give this as sort of a
complimentary welcome gift) which I didn't like
but drank it, so as not to offend them. After an
hour wait, with various 'how much longer' and 'I
had an appointment' app conversations, I was

approached by a lady who was fluent in French but only spoke a little bit of English, but it transpired she didn't even work there as she was the sister of the receptionist who had called her to assist. She therefore knew nothing about the hotel, its operation, safety, technical aspects etc, so she told me wait whilst she found the maintenance engineer. When he arrived, it transpired he only spoke Arabic and nothing else. So the 'sister' then went and found someone (one of the chef's) who could speak French and Arabic so they could translate from Arabic, to French, to the partial English-speaking sister to the only English-speaking auditor. It was like a comedy sketch that went on for hours. I even tried translating straight to Arabic to short cut this process but that wouldn't work as the maintenance guy didn't have his glasses with him so couldn't read the app on my phone. As an example I asked the 'sister', 'what was the date of the last practice fire evacuation' and after this went through the Chinese whisper process from person to person and then back again, the answer come back as 'extinguisher'. It was the longest (4 hours) audit of my life, but we eventually finished it somehow and they were generally ok.

After a quiet night in at the hotel, I was preparing for an early start and a 6-hour drive to Agadir, in the south of the country.

Agadir

Agadir is definitely a tourist destination, very nice indeed. Long beaches, a huge promenade with cafes and restaurants and some very impressive large 5* hotels. It is also a popular stop off for cruise ships that bring hundreds of day trippers to the area. In general it had that 'I am on holiday' feeling to it. I checked in to my hotel which was like any normal beach holiday type hotel, large pool, bar etc and for a very small moment it felt like I was on holiday. Nearly everyone spoke various standards of English which also made everything easier. It was incredibly hot, so I was really looking forward to my upcoming weekend off to enjoy the facilities and amenities Agadir had to offer. After a couple of days of stress-free local driving and more inspections I was finally at Friday night and ready for the weekend to explore the bars and restaurants and try to get some form of tan. The weather over the weekend was not quite as good but it would have still been classed as a 'scorcher' in the UK. My search for Guinness, my favourite tipple, was ongoing and I happily found an Irish bar in the centre that opened later that afternoon. After some food I excitedly entered the premises. As I should have now expected in a Muslim country, alcohol is not exactly on the top of the list of things to provide - even for tourists (a lot of hotels and restaurants didn't sell it), so the Irish bar would certainly struggle to import Guinness from anywhere. They only sold bottles of the local brew and inside there was absolutely no reference to Ireland or anything remotely connected to it. I am not sure how a bar can survive by falsely indicating they are an authentic Irish bar when in fact they are anything but. I eventually found another bar that was showing English football, sold good food and drink and made this my home for 2 days. After all the chaos of the recent few weeks and a lot of driving, it was nice to properly wind down and chill out.

I then received a rather disturbing email from Amazon, asking me if I required any other baby products to go along with my new baby monitor! I spoke with my wife daily so I couldn't imagine that she had 'forgot' to tell me something important so after an urgent phone call to her, luckily, it was all explained. As her office is in the back of the house, she couldn't hear the front doorbell, so this baby device solved the problem. Once my heart rate had returned to normal, I did see the funny side, but for a minute it was panic stations!

After a couple more days auditing, with no major problems, I was packing up and heading to Essaouira, further up the Atlantic coast.

Essaouira

I had been warned that the road from Agadir to Essaouira was in a terrible state and to 'be careful'. It was like off roading for 2 hours, which in a purpose built 4x4 would be fine but not in a Peugeot 308! For long stretches there was no tarmac, just gravel, so every time you turned the wheel the car slid sideways which is not good when all the other cars are doing exactly the same thing. I came across 3 accidents where the simultaneous sliding had come together but everyone was ok, so I continued with my sliding. I drove through some proper out of the way local communities, like Tamanar, which seemed to have more donkeys than cars and as a white Englishman in a white car I was very aware that everyone was stopping what they were doing to gawp at me as I passed. I also needed fuel, not desperately but once I hit a quarter full, I was always on the lookout, so I pulled into the fuel station in Tamanar and waited for someone to come out. No one did, but a guy walked past and told me it only opened on Mondays and Thursdays, that's how remote this place was and given that the main mode of transport was fuelled with straw there was no big demand for it either.

I was driving into Essaouira with a little bit of interpretation as my accommodation there was also in a Riad, which after the relatively nice hotel in Agadir, would be a serious come down and as my sat nav told me to 'park up and walk to my destination' my heart sank deeper.

After a similar process to Tangier, including paying a 'local helper', I found my accommodation. On route though, the smell was terrible. Around my Riad was various market stalls selling fresh food and the aroma was what I imagine an abattoir to smell like, it turned my stomach. After checking into my new broom cupboard (Riad) I ventured out to familiarize myself and to get some food. I had to keep walking to get out of the Medina and away from the smell before I could even look at a menu, and even then, I couldn't face any meat after what I had seen so I ordered a tuna salad. When it arrived, I realised the menu should have said 'Tomato and lettuce, soaked in olive oil and decorated with minute tuna flakes' but luckily it came with bread which helped filled me up. Essaouira is actually very nice, with its long beaches and a busy fishing harbour. I imagine it is where Moroccans go on holiday, but it is also very tourist driven with daily coach tours from Marrakech to keep the market traders happy. After a few more days getting lost and carrying out more uneventful audits I was approaching the weekend again, and this time it was going to be dry and hot!

The beach front is at least a mile long with various bars and restaurants dotted along the front and of course you have the Medina markets to give your ears and nose an adrenaline rush, but apart from that there is very little else to do in Essaouira. So on the Saturday I walked, then sat and then drank, walked some more, sat and drank even more and this continued until I was bright red and more than slightly intoxicated. I again ordered a tuna salad from a different restaurant, one of those where outside they had the pictures of what it looked like. This time the menu should have said 'Massive chunk of tuna with huge portion of salad'. It was lovely and I do not think I have ever been as full after just a salad. I then found a nice bar on the beach front and sat and drank some more whilst the sun went down and then found another bar for another couple of hours until it really was time to go home (broom cupboard) to bed. Sunday was a repeat of Saturday, including the tuna salad, and all in all it was very pleasant weekend.

I woke up about 3am on Monday morning and thought I was going to give birth. The pains in my stomach were doubling me up and I must have spent the rest of the night on the toilet. Now do not forget, I am in a Riad with no windows, air-conditioning or any ventilation and to say the odour in the room was unpleasant is a huge understatement. I cancelled the day's audits and went back to bed, then the toilet, then the bed and this continued for about 24 hours. I do not know what caused it, probably the tuna and excessive alcohol in hot weather, but I am no expert. Just in case it was a stomach bug I cancelled my only audit on Tuesday morning, for obvious reasons, and then prepared to head off to Marrakech for 5 days.

Marrakech

Now I had not eaten anything for 2 days, and even though I was hungry I didn't want to risk anything 'happening' on a 3-hour journey through the remote desert. As I approached Marrakech there was a small supermarket on the side of the road, so I stopped and bought some plain biscuits and more water and headed towards my new broom cupboard. My sat nav was surprisingly not telling me to park up and walk to my destination and was still directing me even though I was only 800 yards from my Riad. I then realised that sometimes sat nav's are bastards. By following the directions I had managed to drive into some alleyways where market traders had to remove their stock to allow me to pass and with no way of turning around I was eventually surrounded by angry people banging on the car and a donkey who didn't look too impressed either. I had nowhere to go and the alleyway was not wide enough for anyone to even walk past me. I was ready to combust and even the donkey was now shouting at me. I was shouting the name of my new broom cupboard, whilst also shouting 'get off the fucking car' but it fell on deaf ears until some young lad of about 18 years of age (aka 'local helper') came over, through the baying crowds, and asked me in English where I was trying to get to. He told me to follow him, backed the angry mob down and he even managed to calm the donkey down! I followed him through the alleyways for about half a mile, stopping people and donkeys until I had gone past and amazingly arrived at my Riad. The relief was incredible, I was happy to offer him 20 Dirham (£5) for his troubles as without him I dread to think how I would have gotten out of that situation. I passed the 20 Dirham through the window and thanked him, but he said, 'I want 150 Dirham' (nearly £35)! I said 20 Dirham is sufficient and thanked him again. 'No, I want 150' he replied. I told him to go away (or words to that effect) and he was getting no more which he eventually understood and disappeared but not before a torrent of abuse was sent my way. I decided at that exact point, that this was my last Riad I was staying in and from now on I would park on the outskirts and get taxis everywhere. The stress was too much. Even the Riad owner could not believe I had drove there.

After checking in, I went out to buy more biscuits and water then returned to sit in my room for the rest of the night in total silence before I started my audits again the next day.

What I had not realised is that I was staying about 100 yards away from a huge mosque. At 4am it was like something had possessed my TV and was shouting at me in Arabic. It was the 'call to prayer' which is a signal from the mosque that it is time to engage in a scheduled prayer ritual. If the guy doing the call to prayer was standing in my room using a megaphone it would not have been any louder. And it goes on for about 20 minutes. Now apparently the loudspeakers are loud enough to be heard 5 kilometres away so you can imagine how loud it was when I was only 100 yards away! I am not religious in the slightest however I have no issue with anybody else believing in whatever they want to believe in, but at 4am on a loudspeaker? At 6am, just when my blood pressure had reduced to just 'very high', it started again!

The next day's audits were all walkable (or taxis refused to take me as it was not possible to drive there) from my broom cupboard and luckily google maps was directing me very well until I got quite close. It is very hard to describe the locations of the Riads, even though I have already tried, as it was alleyway after alleyway, then some doors that all look the same, some have numbers on, and some do not. Looking for my last audit of the day and having gone as far as google could take me, I was stood at the front of one dead-end alleyway that had 3 doors when I was approached by a 'local helper'. I told him that I didn't need any help as I was at my location but thanked him anyway. He stayed next to me and again I politely asked him to go as I did not need him. He muttered something like' English pig' and left. I ignored him and moved into the alleyway and was checking the paperwork for the address again, when he come back with a friend and they both evidently started mocking the fact that I was still there by laughing and pointing at my paperwork and then started to point at my lap top on my shoulder, whilst his friend moved behind me. I had by now had enough, it had probably been building since I arrived in Morocco, and I flipped. Without thinking of the consequences, I angrily screamed into his face to 'fuck off' and turned to his friend who got the same treatment whilst I was making it very obvious that if they wanted to take this further, I was happy to proceed. In hindsight this was a very dumb move, but I was cornered in a dead end and thought I would fight fire with fire. Luckily, it worked and they both ran off, but I was also aware that could have ended very differently, and they may have just gone to get some more friends, so I needed to move quickly. One of the 3 doors suddenly opened, probably to see what all the shouting was about, and to my relief it was the Riad that I was looking for. They let me in, and I carried out the audit after a sit down to recompose myself. I was a little apprehensive when I left but the' local helpers' were nowhere to be seen. I went straight back to my hotel for the night and watched TV, whilst still only eating biscuits as I was still feeling a bit queasy.

I again woke at 4am with the relentless, very loud, warbling of the call to prayer. I found out later that even some hotels and Riads had speakers installed that were linked to the Mosque speakers, maybe so even the stone deaf could hear it!

I also realised I was very hungry as all I had eaten in 3 days was dry biscuits. My audits that day were right in the centre of the tourist part of Marrakech, just by the main square of Jemaa el-Fnaa, so I hoped there would somewhere I would recognise so I could get some proper food. After getting a taxi for a few miles to another medina, then walking for ages through more alleyways with live chickens, donkeys, scooters and the world's largest population of flies, I completed my first audit. I bought some water as it was so hot and humid and was standing just outside the medina and I thinking I should video the area so when I got home it would be easier to describe to everyone how chaotic it really was there, when I could see some sort of trauma unfolding in front of me. It appeared that some guy was chasing a taxi whilst shouting at the top of his voice in Arabic, then he stopped to pick something up, then carried on chasing the taxi. After chatting to the guy next me, before I had chance to replay my video, it all become clear what had happened. He said It was normal practice that once you had completed your journey you paid the taxi once you were stood outside of it (not that I had been doing this). This guy had gotten out of the car and got his wallet out to pay the taxi driver when the driver grabbed his wallet and drove off. He obviously took out what he wanted and threw it back on the road before speeding off and I had all this caught on video! I decided to walk the 15 minutes or so into the centre of Marrakech as it was probably easier, and maybe safer after what I had just seen, than getting a taxi. I arrived at the main tourist square and again the whole area was chaotic, from performing monkeys, snake charmers, tourists surrounded by 'local helpers' and what seemed like an organised gang who were picking and choosing which female tourists they were going to try and 'help'. I sat and watched this for about half an hour and my initial feelings were correct as one by one these 'helpers' would return and give the 'chief helper' the money they had collected. Then the process would repeat again and again. Now I appreciate I probably won't ever get, or want, a job at the Marrakech tourist board (especially if they read this), but if I did, this practice of harassment would be addressed. I have recently read some reviews from Marrakech and there are plenty of females who would concur with my initial assessment. I left the main square and I wasn't disappointed when I could see KFC not far away, so I went in, ordered half of the menu and sat in relative calm whilst I enjoyed my first proper food for 3 days. There are probably loads of lovely restaurants in Marrakech but having seen first-hand where they buy their produce from, I really did not fancy any of them. After one more audit I got a taxi, from the central taxi rank, back to near my Riad and settled down for another night.

After my 4am and 6am wake up calls I headed out for more audits and was also starting to appreciate the beauty of some of the better Riads. The smaller and evidently cheaper ones that I was staying in are basic broom cupboards with limited character whilst the nicer ones are like mini palaces, with swimming pools and the hospitality is second to none. 'When you stay here, this isn't a Riad, it is your home' was one owners' explanation and you could tell his prime role was for tourists to enjoy the whole experience. They also have no menus; you just tell the owner what you fancy for your dinner and he will go and purchase it all locally and cook it for you. You still must walk through endless, unlit, mazey alleyways to come and go though and a 'local helper' would never be far away to 'help' you out. At night-time though, especially if you are alone, it was an even more intimidating place to be. After more KFC I headed back for my last night's sleep before an early start and a 6-hour drive to Fes, in the north.

I wanted out of Marrakech as soon as possible so after my 4am wakeup call I was happy to get up and get going. The Riad owner was also up and he graciously helped me navigate through the alleyways until I got to a proper road and the relief was huge. Even though I had a long drive ahead, I felt free and relaxed again.

Fes

Driving through the desert is a weird experience as you could literally see no one for hours, apart from the toll booth employees and at the service stations. After stopping a few times for fuel etc, and by-passing Casablanca, I was probably about 2 hours outside Fes when I was stopped at a security check point. By now I have passed through lots of these without getting stopped, apart from asking for directions, and I have no idea what the officer said to me but once he realised that I was English he waved me through. Security in Morocco was very visible and even the hotels (not Riads) had airport type scanners you must walk through. It had not struck me before, but the terrorist element was obviously a severe threat and they were doing everything they could to be as visible as possible to combat that danger. A couple of days later, when I was back in Casablanca, the police raided an apartment and found weapons, ammunition, chemical bombs, and flags belonging to the well-known terror group, ISIS, just before an imminent attack. 7 people were arrested.

My hotel in Fes turned out to be in a Raid, even though the address didn't indicate this, and once I realised, I changed it to a proper hotel on the outskirts. It is a well-known but very basic chain of hotels, but it felt like a 5* hotel after the Riads I had been staying in. The audits over the next couple of days were a mixture of Riads and all the chaos that comes with them as well as ultra-luxurious 5* properties on the outskirts of Fes. I also found a fantastic, large and very modern designer shopping mall with world famous brands and coffee shops. It was a bizarre mix of culture but one that was most welcome and my trips to the mall were a taste of home which by now I was really missing.

One morning after leaving my hotel I was following my sat nav to the nearest part of the medina I could park up at before another Riad inspection, when I stopped at some traffic lights. A scooter pulled up next to me and the helmetless rider asked me where I was going. I told him I was fine and drove off as the lights turned green. At the next set he was there again and again he told me he would like to help me. I could not get rid of him and he followed me all the way to the car park, even after I had switched the engine off he was still by my window. He eventually left when he realised that he was not going to get his 'helpers' fee, mainly because I didn't need any help! Now I may be tarnishing good local people who just genuinely want to help tourists, but if I need help, I will ask. To follow somebody whilst riding a scooter for about 2 miles is harassment however 'helpful' he was trying to be, but this did mean the 'local helpers' were also mobile!

After another day auditing with no problems, apart from the usual issues of getting lost trying to find Riads etc I headed back to the shopping mall as I had previously noticed a Pizza hut was in there and I couldn't get 'pizza' out of my head ever since so I satisfied that craving, did a bit of shopping and headed back to the hotel for my last night in Fes and my budget paradise hotel. Randomly, as a side note, it is also worth mentioning that I did not see one person wearing a 'Fez' the whole time I was there which disappointed me slightly.

After packing up and checking out of the hotel I had a few audits to complete then I was heading back to Casablanca, again, for 3 nights.

Casablanca (take 3)

My hotel this time was on the opposite side of Casablanca that I had been to previously, quite close to the seafront and very nice indeed. I felt like doing a Macaulay Culkin when he was 'Home Alone' in New York and start jumping up and down on the bed and ordering the whole menu from room service. It was by far the nicest hotel I had stayed in since arriving in Morocco, but the area it was in looked a little bit dodgy to say the least. The front desk told me not to take out any more money than I needed, leave my passport in the safe and take my room card with me so I could produce it if stopped by the police. Well that was reassuring and confirmed my first thoughts. As it was now Friday night and I had the weekend off I planned my weekend activities, which was, as usual, generally walking, eating and drinking. During the drive into Casablanca I had spotted a shopping mall about a 3-mile walk from my hotel, all the way down the sea front so that was Saturday's activity and the views, and the weather were fantastic.

It also amazes me that however poor little villages, towns or even the larger cities are and the derelict state of many of their homes, one thing you could always rely on is a fantastic modern mosque with stunning architecture standing proud. The mosque by the seafront at Casablanca is absolutely amazing, but a few hundred yards away the area is quite evidently run down and very poorly maintained. It does beg the question where their priorities are and where they should be?

I spent a few hours in the mall, shopping, eating and drinking, then headed back to my hotel. About 50 yards away from my hotel I noticed an 'English bar' and as I had walked over 6 miles in 30-degree heat, I was virtually on my knees so went inside for some 'refreshments'. As expected, this English pub was nothing of the sort and I imagine it was owned by a Mr Mustafa Mohammed English and hence why it was called the English bar. It was a small local pub in a Muslim country that by religious definition don't drink alcohol, so I sat in there on my own for about 5 hours until I was 'totally refreshed' and best pals with the 'Mo Salah' loving bar owner. Luckily, I didn't have far to stagger home although in that drunken state I was convinced I was being followed but by that stage my imagination had run riot so there was probably 'loads of them' on horseback, with guns.

After waking up on the Sunday with a monster hangover I decided to walk in the opposite direction to the previous day and headed towards the Casablanca market, about a mile away to clear my head. I am sorry I did as it was more than 2 miles away and was a typical noisy chaotic closed in market, where the various foods on offer created an odour that wasn't doing me any favours. I did a bit of haggling and bought a few designer t-shirts for next to nothing ('these are very genuine sir and not a copy') and then found some quality anti-hangover food (KFC) and then returned to my hotel for an early night.

Unbelievably, after an early Monday morning audit I was heading back to my least favourite place in the world (at this point), Marrakech.

Marrakech (take 2)

After another 3-hour drive through the desert I arrived at Marrakech and to my relief I was in a normal hotel on the outskirts and it instantly gave me a different perspective to Marrakech. This was modern, clean, and the totally opposite from the chaos of the centre. My audits were spaced out over the week with only one or two a day to complete and the appointments were all in some of the nicest hotels I have ever been to, also on the outskirts of the city. Huge 5* properties where some of the rooms even had private butlers and some of the most impressive architecture I have ever seen. Now if this were the area of Marrakech you have visited you would argue that there is nowhere better in the world and that Marrakech is fantastic, and it would be hard not to disagree. It was a great week to be honest with lots of quality audits, sunbathing around the pool and the food and drink in the hotel was also fantastic. Even walking around the adjoining retail park and supermarket was a pleasant experience and the people were genuinely nice. If I ever go back to Marrakech, and that is a big 'if', I would certainly head to this part, on the West side of the city. If you are staying in any area of Marrakech you obviously have to take a trip into the centre, just to experience the carnage of it all (otherwise known as local culture), but you need to have your wits about you and research as much as you can so you are as prepared as you can be.

As a big rugby fan I had tried to follow the rugby union world cup from Japan as much as I could, but bearing in mind the time difference, the fact that rugby isn't exactly at the top of Morocco's television sporting priorities and I was also working, it was difficult to watch as much as I wanted to. It also depended whether my hotel room even had a tv! As luck would have it though, I was staying in a nice hotel, with the day off and England were playing New Zealand in the semi-final. It did mean I had to get up at 7am to watch it but I wouldn't have missed it for the world. I tuned into the only channel that was showing it, which was a French TV station with Arabic subtitles, so I obviously turned the volume right down but at least I could watch it live. It was an epic game and I was really getting into it, shouting and cheering, probably swearing a lot and clapping. I can only imagine what someone outside my door would have been thinking, with an Englishman shouting for 80 minutes, 'get in' 'push' 'keep going' 'the hooker is useless' and then clapping and cheering. We won though and it felt fantastic to beat probably the best team in the competition and I was already looking forward to watching the final, in my own house in England a week later.

After a final night in Marrakech and one more morning audit I was heading back to, for the 4th time, Casablanca.

Casablanca (take 4)

As I entered my fifth week of driving in Morocco,
I think I had adapted to it pretty well (both
myself and the car were still in one piece
anyway) and I was by now also joining in with the
relentless and pointless pressing of the car horn
whenever I pleased, just like the locals. If you are
15 cars back at traffic lights and they turn green,
you press your horn to let the car in front know
they can go. But they cannot move as there is a
car in front of them that also cannot move, so
they press their horn. The cars behind have also
clocked the green light so they are pressing
away. So with approximately 30-40 stationary
cars all pressing their horn there was a total wall
of noise and totally pointless. This was repeated
at every set of lights and if someone had the
audacity to stop at a pedestrian crossing to let
someone cross, it was repeated 2-fold. Now as I
entered Casablanca there was something new, a
traffic policeman in the middle of the road with a
whistle, directing traffic. The issue was he was
telling people, by hand signals, to go even if the
lights were on red, and stopping traffic if they
were on green, whilst blowing his whistle
relentlessly. The noise was incredible. I imagine
someone, somewhere, who has maybe never
even been to the centre of Casablanca, had
dreamt this up as a solution to the traffic

problems. It only added to the trauma and I was glad when I eventually got to my hotel where for an hour, I sat in total silence staring at the walls. The following morning I arrived back to where it all began, with what should have been my first audit nearly 5 weeks ago, but this time I was there when I should have been. After a few more inspections I settled down for the night with a few beers in the hotel and a subtitled version of Die Hard on the TV.

El Jadida

I realised that tomorrow was going to be my last night in Morocco. In the morning I had a 2-hour drive to El Jadida, further down the coast for my final audit in a huge posh complex on the sea front, then a 2 hour drive back up to my hotel in chaotic Casablanca, then a 30 minute drive back down to the airport the following morning for my flight home. This made no sense to me, but someone in the UK office who had evidently never been to Morocco and couldn't read maps or google had dreamt this up as a logistically great plan so I made the judgement call to book into, and pay for myself, the hotel I was auditing. It was one of my better decisions as the hotel was awesome, pure luxury. After completing the audit I checked in with a 'I have finished' elation that I can't quite describe. After catching some final Moroccan sun around the huge pool, I showered and headed out for a sort of last night celebration. After eating in the massively overpriced but delicious buffet I headed into the adjacent hotel casino where they were showing a live Liverpool football game on a huge screen, surrounded by lots of Mo Salah fans. When they realised that I was from Liverpool, once again I suddenly had lots of new best friends who wanted to know everything about the city and the football club. They already knew everything about Mo Salah.

After the game had finished, I put some Dirham into one of the slot machines and instantly won about £200. This more than paid for my last night of luxury so after a few more beers headed back to my room for my last night's sleep in Morocco. It was the perfect ending to, especially at some points, a very difficult, demanding and stressful trip.

After sleeping like a baby in a bed the size of Gibraltar, I packed up and headed to the airport. After driving over 3500 kilometres together, me and my Peugeot car were glad to see the back of each other, thankfully though we had both survived.

Homeward bound

As I was waiting in the departure lounge, I started to reflect on my time in North Africa. The culture difference between the UK and Morocco is huge and certainly contributed to my difficulties early on. I had little or no time to research the country due to only having a few days' notice before departure, nor did I plan the route or book my accommodation as this was done centrally in the UK by someone who evidently had no idea of the countries layout, or its Medina and Riad arrangement. I would never get used to Riads as a form of hotel accommodation, but I was glad I had the opportunity to experience them as they are totally different to anything that I have stayed in before. Washing and drying my clothes was a logistical nightmare as I was either not in the hotel long enough, or in a Riad with no way of drying them, but I somehow managed to always have clean clothes. Not speaking the local language was difficult, but I somehow managed to live and work there without speaking a word of French or Arabic and at some points this deficiency also provided a few laughs along the way. Driving in the main cities was horrific from start to finish, but elsewhere it was a relaxing pleasure. I got into some very close, and sometimes scary, scrapes but I survived and learnt from them. The weather and the heat made working difficult and unpleasant sometimes, but I eventually acclimatised and enjoyed it and having a bit of a tan to go home with was nice. Though I spoke to my wife daily, I realised I had missed home in a way I hadn't before. Adapting to, and eventually embracing some of those differences took time but overall, I was glad I experienced living and working in Morocco. I was also pretty proud of myself that I was totally out of my comfort zone, whilst alone, and completing a difficult schedule of hotel inspections.

After another Air Maroc flight to Amsterdam, more airport fast food, and a very quiet flight to Liverpool I was met in the airport arrival lounge by my beautiful wife who I had missed massively.

After 5 weeks in Morocco, I was glad to be home.

Conclusion

Do I still think it is the dream job? Absolutely. Does something always fuck it up? Definitely! But the experiences you get from doing this role are second to none and even the bad moments are memories and knowledge for the future, with plenty of lessons learnt by all concerned. I was not on holiday, I was working and that isn't always fun and laughter in any job you have, but you try to get the best out of it that you can.

Better planning, with more experienced planners, in the UK office would undoubtably save time and money, whilst ensuring the risk to the auditor is kept to an absolute minimum with the knowledge that sometimes, what works on paper does not always work in reality. Should I have been put in some of the situations I ended up in? Of course not. Did the UK office plan for me to be in those situations? Of course not, but some of them could have definitely been avoided.

If I had longer than the normal 2-3 days' notice to plan and research the countries I was visiting, I would have been far better prepared and potentially would have saved me a lot of grief and uncertainty. Likewise if I spoke different languages it would have help, but who knows what country I was going to be sent to?

I found changing a small amount of currency in the airport I had just landed in was by far the easiest, but probably not the cheapest, method of having local cash on me at all times and also saved the hassle of trying to find somewhere in resort. This was even more important if you were going from country to country to country as you could change all your now not required currency into the new required one.

Health and Safety standards around the world differ massively and it was never the intention to enforce UK standards on other countries but there has to be, and there is, a 'minimum standard' if hoteliers are expected to accept travellers and holiday makers from around the world. The technical documentation that has been produced are only guidelines though, that some hoteliers follow to the letter and are still willing to improve, whilst some totally disregard them and lie to your face during the inspection. Different countries have different regulations that do not even meet these guidelines, so therefore the hotelier is unlikely to change anything as they are already 'complying with local regulations'.
It certainly made the job more interesting though and the highs generally exceeded the lows.

Thank you for taking the time to read about my experiences and I hope you can take with you some hints and tips of what to do, or not to do, onto your next journey.

Lyndon Tillary

Printed in Great Britain
by Amazon

81304180R10096